Timberline Country

D1603322

Timberline
Country

THE SIERRA HIGH ROUTE

by Steve Roper

SIERRA CLUB BOOKS   San Francisco

The Sierra Club, founded in 1892 by John Muir, has devoted itself to the study and protection of the earth's scenic and ecological resources—mountains, wetlands, woodlands, wild shores and rivers, deserts and plains. The publishing program of the Sierra Club offers books to the public as a nonprofit educational service in the hope that they may enlarge the public's understanding of the Club's basic concerns. The point of view expressed in each book, however, does not necessarily represent that of the Club. The Sierra Club has some fifty chapters coast to coast, in Canada, Hawaii, and Alaska. For information about how you may participate in its programs to preserve wilderness and the quality of life, please address inquiries to Sierra Club, 530 Bush Street, San Francisco, CA 94108.

Quote on page 249 is from *The Dharma Bums* by Jack Kerouac. Copyright © 1958 by Jack Kerouac. Reprinted by permission of Viking Penguin Inc.

Library of Congress Cataloging in Publication Data
Roper, Steve.
   Timberline country.
   Includes index.
   1. Backpacking—Sierra Nevada Mountains (Calif. and Nev.)—Guide-books. 2. Hiking—Sierra Nevada Mountains (Calif. and Nev.)—Guide-books. 3. Sierra Nevada Mountains (Calif. and Nev.)—Guide-books. I. Title.
GV199.42.S55R66   917.94′40433   82–714
ISBN 0–87156–298–7 (pbk.)   AACR2

Cover and book design by Paula Schlosser
Illustrations by Chris Romano
Maps by Nancy Warner

Printed in the United States of America
10 9 8 7 6 5 4 3 2 1

Contents

Much of the charm of the mountains depends upon the absolute harmony of all that is there. There is no intrusive foreign thing in them; there is no inappropriate thing; there is no vulgar thing. They do not insolently thrust in your face silly placards . . . ; they do not disfigure themselves with lying real-estate signs; the names of no political candidates insult the trees; there are no yelping curs, blatant voices, or jangling street-cars; there is no odor of underground horrors or discomfort of dirty crowds. In the mountains all is large, quiet, pure, strong, dignified; there all is beautiful; each thing is a perfectly appropriate part of that unity which we call nature. . . . All is wholesome to the body, interesting to the mind, and agreeable to the senses. And the state of mind they tend to put us in may be called poetic.

Bolton Coit Brown. From
the January 1897 issue of
the *Sierra Club Bulletin.*

Preface

DURING THE COURSE of several summers, I hiked every segment of the Sierra High Route at least once, gathering the descriptive material that forms the bulk of this guidebook. On most of these forays into the heart of the range I was accompanied by friends who, without overt complaining, tolerated my seemingly random wanderings through the subalpine landscape. Each of the following companions became intimately familiar with one or more sections of the route: Gilles Corcos, Marjorie Gelus, Dick Long, Larry Marino, Allen Steck, and Jim Wilson. To these friends—and especially to my wife, Kathy, who accompanied me on two-thirds of the route —I wish to express my appreciation. Their suggestions often led to an improvement in the course of the High Route, and their obvious enchantment with the scenery confirmed my own feelings.

Quoted material is used throughout the book, especially in the historical overview. Whenever the source of a quotation is omitted, the reader generally can assume the source to be the *Sierra Club Bulletin,* usually the annual issue immediately following the trip described.

In the interest of readability I have chosen to simplify certain technical details. For instance, I routinely imply that the High Route—and therefore the Sierra Nevada—runs in a north-south direction. The range, like the Pacific shoreline, actually tilts about thirty degrees off that convenient axis, trending in a direction that more closely approximates north-northwest by south-southeast. I am aware also that the typical Sierra rock is not really granite; geologists use such words as granodiorite and quartz monzonite to describe the range's common rock. But, as Stephen Whitney has written in his excellent volume, *A Sierra Club Naturalist's Guide to the Sierra Nevada,* "the word *granite* has a long history of popular use predating the more restricted definition assigned to it by geologists." In such place names as Red's Meadow and Devil's Postpile, I have used apostrophes even though they are missing in many guidebooks and all the official government maps. Cartographers dislike apostrophes for esoteric reasons, but I have heeded David Brower's thirty-year-old advice: "Until someone can marshall sensible reasons against our doing so, we'll use the apostrophe just the way it should be used to make sense." Finally, when exact elevations are not indicated on the topo maps, I have approximated them. A High Route pass, for example, might lie above the 11,280-foot contour line but below the next line, the one representing 11,360 feet. Technically, this pass should be shown as lying at 11,280+ feet, but I prefer to use the less awkward figure of, in this case, 11,300 feet.

Introduction

T HE TIMBERLINE COUNTRY of California's Sierra Nevada is dominated by five elements: meadowlands, gnarled trees, water, stone, and a cobalt sky occasionally augmented by towering cumulus clouds. In this austere landscape, backpackers who travel along the Sierra High Route—a rugged alternative to the John Muir Trail—can forget the outside world and concentrate solely on moving cross-country from one pristine campsite to another.

Although the justly popular John Muir Trail traverses this fascinating timberline country on occasion, it frequently descends west into heavily forested regions in order to circumvent the great spur ridges that so often jut out from the main Sierra crest. These diversions from what I regard as the range's finest terrain become especially annoying in the northern half of the High Sierra, for here the famed path traverses relatively lackluster country for many miles.

It occurred to me some five years ago that if I scouted the range carefully I might be able to piece together a continuous route that would remain longer in timberline

5

country than does the John Muir Trail. Such a route, if feasible, would offer adventurous hikers an opportunity to visit superb country while simultaneously avoiding the multitudes of backpackers who prefer well-marked trails. In subsequent years I explored hundreds of cirques and ridges, ending up in more cul-de-sacs than I care to remember. But eventually I evolved a marvelous 195-mile route that remains in close proximity to timberline, avoids major trails whenever possible, and yet requires no particular mountaineering skills. Almost all of what I call the Sierra High Route—or High Route for short—lies between 9,000 and 11,500 feet, that subalpine region fortuitously sandwiched between the dense western-slope forest and the ubiquitous granite blocks of the alpine zone.

Backpackers must not regard the High Route as an actual *trail.* Except for the sections where it follows existing paths, the High Route traverses such rocky country that traces of human passage remain virtually indetectable. In this rugged landscape there is no "correct" route to hike, and each person naturally will choose a slightly different way. Similarly, in the far more fragile meadowlands through which the High Route occasionally passes, so many choices are available that paths are unlikely to be created except at a few locations where the terrain forces hikers to funnel into one specific area. Even here, without the destructive hooves of pack animals to create deep trenches, the paths should remain inconspicuous. High Route adventurers will not be put off by the lack of an actual trail, since much of the singular joy of cross-country travel lies in wandering through the timberline country as the pioneers did—wondering what the next turn will reveal. Maintaining the pristine, trailless character of the High Route requires a conscious effort on the part of backpackers, and later in the introduction I discuss methods of preserving this fragile landscape.

The High Route begins in lovely Kings Canyon, that Yosemite-like gorge in the southern Sierra. I chose this location because it was the chief goal of the pioneers who, around the turn of the century, sought a high mountain route, passable to pack animals, from Yosemite southward. (Chapter 1 relates some of the exploits of these pioneers.) For two reasons, I believe the High Route is more practical when traveled from south to north, and it is so described. First, less snow falls in the southern half of the range than in the northern half; thus, intrepid hikers who plan to do the entire route will reach the zone of heavier snowpack later in the season, when the winter's snow will have had additional time to melt. Second, by traveling northward, hikers generally walk away from the sun instead of into its blinding rays.

Climbing immediately from Kings Canyon some 6,000 feet to the Monarch Divide, the High Route then parallels this long ridge until it abuts the Sierra crest near Mather Pass. Three exceptionally lovely basins are encountered in the next few dozen miles: Palisade, Dusy, and Evolution. After crossing the Glacier Divide, the High Route mean-

ders across vast Humphreys Basin, then traverses the Bear
Lakes region, the Mono Recesses, and the Silver Divide.
Farther north, the route follows Mammoth Crest for a few
miles before dropping abruptly to Devil's Postpile National Monument. The High Route then threads through
the Ritter Range and enters Yosemite National Park via
a remote pass near Foerster Peak. From this point the
hiker follows seldom-traveled paths through Yosemite's
backcountry to Tuolumne Meadows. The final segment of
the High Route closely parallels the Sierra crest, crossing
it three times before reaching the route's northern terminus at Twin Lakes, near the village of Bridgeport.

Although the name "Sierra High Route" is mine, I
make no claim for having pioneered a single step of the
route. I first tramped through the Range of Light in 1954,
a few decades too late to have explored virgin territory.
Certain sections of what was to become the High Route
have been described briefly in various guidebooks. On
other segments I came across footprints and cairns, rather
indisputable evidence that I was not first. Yet the conception of a continuous timberline route—for humans, not
pack animals—is probably mine, at least on paper.

Although I was delighted personally with my "discovery" of the High Route, I agonized for more than a year
about whether or not to make its details public. The untrammeled nature of the timberline region has attracted
me almost every summer for nearly thirty years; why, I

thought, should I advertise this paradise in a guidebook that would encourage numerous people to visit an area they otherwise might miss? Motives prove difficult to analyze, and, as Karl Marx once wrote, "the road to Hell is paved with good intentions." But in the end my incorrigible optimism prevailed; I am convinced that those backpackers capable of traversing the High Route's rugged and austere terrain will be the very ones who will leave no trace of their passage. I devoutly hope I am correct in this conviction.

My chief concern while laying out the course of the High Route was to avoid excessively troublesome terrain. The difficulty of the 195-mile trek is necessarily subjective, for although mountaineers will find the route easy, neophytes could well have a rough time. Three categories adequately describe the type of travel encountered: *trail walking, easy cross-country walking,* and *rugged cross-country travel.*

Trail walking, often necessary on the High Route unless the hiker wishes to struggle over contrived routes, comprises nearly half the journey. The traveler follows the John Muir Trail for a total of thirty miles and far more obscure paths for another sixty-five miles or so.

The great majority of the High Route—if one thinks in terms of time, not distance—traverses trailless but easy country. Meadowlands and granite slabs make up much of this distance, but solid, gently angled talus also is included in this category. ("Talus," as used in this book, refers to blocks of rock measuring a foot or more across their longest dimension.) Few persons experienced in trail walking will have trouble with this type of terrain if they take their time.

A small percentage of the High Route's distance falls into the category of onerous travel, usually involving steep and loose talus. These sections, most often encountered when crossing major east-west ridges, are not far in distance, but the hiker should expect to spend an hour or two on each crossing. No particular rockclimbing skills are required—and no ropes need be carried—but unsteady beginners with unwieldy packs will be ill at ease on such terrain. For this reason I strongly suggest that potential High Route travelers, if inexperienced on this type of terrain, spend a few weeks in a less rugged part of the High Sierra prior to committing themselves to any lengthy portion of the trek. Later in the book I include a few hints on how to make cross-country walking of this type more pleasurable—or, phrased another way, less miserable.

Because of this occasionally rugged terrain, no group ever should set forth on the High Route without an experienced leader. Among other skills, this person must be well versed in interpreting topographic maps; be proficient at scrambling up and down class 3 rock; know first-aid procedures thoroughly; and be able to recognize quickly the often subtle signs that indicate a less experienced hiker may be in trouble. By moving slowly and lending a helping hand on a few rough spots, an experienced leader can safely shepherd a flock of novice mountaineers over any portion of the High Route.

Most backpackers will prefer to travel the High Route in sections rather than in its entirety, a month-long trek. Therefore, I have divided the route into five segments, each of which forms a chapter of the book. The end points of each segment either abut roads or are easily accessible from nearby ones. Each of the five segments will take most backpackers five or six days to hike, but it must be kept in mind that this estimate does not include the time spent approaching the High Route, enjoying rest days and side trips, or returning to the starting point or a bus stop. Thus, one easily might spend an entire two-week vacation accomplishing each segment.

I have subdivided each route chapter into six sections. The chapter opens with an overview highlighting the most interesting geographical and historical aspects of the route segment. An accompanying diagram enumerates the specific maps needed en route. These maps, excerpted from topographic sheets, will be found near the end of the book.

Following this general description is an "Approaches" section, which describes how to reach either end of the segment. This section also outlines interesting loop trips that will enable the hiker to return to the starting point via a different route. These circuits should appeal to hikers who leave cars at a roadhead near either end of the segment.

The bulk of each chapter describes the course of the High Route in general terms; specific directions rarely are given in hopes that hikers will be adventurous enough to try the numerous possible variations.

A brief section called "Reversing the Route" follows; it is designed to aid nonconformists planning to travel "backwards" along the High Route. Only places where the north-to-south traveler might encounter difficulties are described; details of the remainder of the route can be extrapolated from the main route description.

Next comes a section on "Alternate Routes." Since the hiker hardly is required to follow the High Route slavishly in order to travel through remarkable timberline country, these secondary routes, paralleling or diverting from the High Route, should be considered by all travelers. Some of these alternate routes involve crossing more difficult terrain than is found on the High Route itself; some entail less strenuous walking. All of these alternates prove interesting, and some reach extremely remote regions well worth visiting. Furthermore, using alternate routes will help to reduce the impact on the landscape of a potentially increased number of hikers.

Finally, a section called "Mountaineering en Route" describes enjoyable, nontechnical climbs that can be reached easily from the High Route. Venturesome hikers will enjoy remarkable panoramas from these summits.

Rudiments of Cross-Country Travel

As mentioned earlier, much of the High Route involves cross-country travel, a type of hiking significantly different from normal trail walking. Perhaps the greatest dissimilarity between the two types concerns the walker's rhythm. The consistent, relaxing strides favored by those who travel well-maintained trails are replaced, in rugged terrain, by irregular movements of the feet and continual body shifts that alter balance.

These important adjustments of rhythm and technique cannot be learned from a book, as competence in any sport is attained only by practice. While the rudiments of such city sports as tennis or bowling can be learned relatively quickly because of readily available facilities and instructors, few persons have the time, opportunity, or patience to practice cross-country hiking. Rather, the tendency is for the neophyte to go out and *do* it, solving problems as they arise, without benefit of formal instruction. This casual approach seems admirable to me, for in the end it proves more rewarding to discover techniques on one's own than to be told at every juncture what one is doing wrong. Still, cross-country hiking of the variety encountered on the more rugged portions of the High Route can be made safer and more enjoyable by absorbing the small number of basic lessons a book can furnish. The advice that follows is given with one overriding thought in mind: a trip without traumas is bound to be a pleasurable one.

Perhaps the prime piece of advice for beginners is to start hiking early each day and move slowly, but inexorably, toward the next campsite. Unpleasant experiences often result from being tired and pressed for time at the end of a strenuous day. Don't attempt long distances at first, especially if the terrain exceeds 11,000 feet, where the thin air adversely affects the stamina and judgment of unacclimated hikers. In short, those backpackers who are not compelled to race the sinking sun are more likely to enjoy their adventure.

However carefully one plans the itinerary, the day's journey will not be carefree if one is burdened with inferior or unnecessary equipment. Although the cross-country hiker's gear closely approximates that of the trail walker, the traveler should reevaluate his or her equipment with the more demanding terrain in mind. The two most important items to reexamine are boots and packs.

Lightweight boots suitable for trail walking may not give the talus walker enough support; indeed, they may even fall apart before the journey is completed. Boots constructed with heavier materials and thicker soles will prove superior on much of the High Route's rugged terrain. (Incidentally, lug soles once were thought to be indispensable for mountain travel; yet boots with smooth rubber or composition soles work equally well in High Route terrain and are preferable to lug soles because they don't tear apart the earth underfoot with such alarming efficiency.)

Regardless of the weight carried, packs constructed with aluminum tubing are usually top-heavy, and as the hiker lurches through talus, the rigid load can shift abruptly and throw him or her off balance. Doug Robinson, editor of the latest edition of *Starr's Guide to the John Muir Trail,* aptly calls these frame packs "equilibrium destroyers." Frameless packs—or packs with nonrigid internal frames—prove far superior for cross-country travel because they cannot shift independently of the body. The hiker in the market for a new pack should consider the frameless styles. In addition to their nonshifting characteristics, frameless packs admirably substitute as daypacks, a boon to hikers who plan side trips while on a backpacking journey. It must be admitted that frameless packs have one drawback: they are not as comfortable as their rigid counterparts. Resting directly against the body, they quickly trap the sweat from one's back, thus causing a hot, sticky feeling relieved only by removing the burden.

Break camp at dawn, strap on sturdy boots and a comfortable pack, and all will go well, right? Hardly, for the traveler soon faces the first of the myriad daily decisions —which way to go? The general directions given in this guide are intended solely to free the hiker from having to make *major* decisions. Solving a specific routefinding problem is such an enjoyable and rewarding exercise that it would be inappropriate to describe the High Route step-by-step, even if this were possible in a pocket-sized guidebook designed to be carried while hiking the route.

And don't forget that such decision-making comprises a pleasurable ingredient of cross-country travel.

It follows, then, that at least one member of the party must be willing and able to make routefinding decisions at every stage of the journey. This person must learn to plan ahead, not only for the next few steps, but sometimes for half a mile at a time. Which side of the lake has less talus? Which of several notches on the ridge above appears easiest, and what might lie on the other side—a cliff or easy ledges? These judgments are hardly of a cosmic nature; a "wrong" choice might result in a brief delay or an unnecessary elevation change of a few feet. Nevertheless, leaders proud of their routefinding abilities will strive to avoid even minor errors, with the subtle result that group members should feel less tired and thus more animated at the end of each day.

Becoming competent at finding the most desirable route, the traveler soon learns, is chiefly a matter of practice. Still, a few strategies can be learned in advance. One easily learned tactic involves scanning the upcoming terrain, especially from high places, and memorizing specific landmarks. Such signposts, of course, will change both in shape and prominence as the hiker approaches them.

Understanding something of the Sierra's geography also can enable the leader to choose the most appropriate route. For instance, willows often choke valleys below 9,000 feet. Talus tends to be unstable above 11,500 feet. The High Route traverses the zone between these two elevations as much as possible, but during approaches to —and departures from—the route, such potentially unpleasant terrain may be avoided if the problem is recognized in advance. In the same vein, the traveler should be aware that north- and east-facing slopes usually are steeper than their opposite sides and also can harbor dangerous snow and ice. Thus, when traveling north on the High Route (with such slopes hidden from view), knowledge of this fact can help hikers to traverse problematic places on their easier sides.

Even though much of the High Route passes through gentle terrain where the walking resembles that done on a trail, the traveler occasionally encounters rugged spots where the feet must be placed with precision, both for efficiency's sake and to avoid injury. This technique is especially necessary when clambering through steep, loose talus, by far the most demanding terrain on the High Route. Variously sized boulders, sharp-edged and stacked like dominoes, blanket the higher regions of the Sierra. The traveler frequently comes across granite blocks so precariously perched that it seems a phantom's breath could send them tumbling downward. While a nudge from a careless hiker's pack might be all it takes to send such a boulder into the void, more often it is the hiker's foot that is responsible. If a rock is dislodged, the perpetrator can suffer a frightening and painful tumble, simultaneously cascading stones onto hikers below.

To avoid such a traumatic incident, simply bypass any

loose-looking rocks. When ascending talus, this proves rather easy to do, for by taking a few moments to test suspicious boulders, it is possible to choose the most secure holds. But when heading downhill, it is difficult to determine if a prospective foothold is stable, since gravity and momentum—those inexorable demons—dictate that the hiker make abrupt movements over terrain that cannot be studied in advance. For this reason, the descent of a talus slope proves more demanding than its ascent and merits further discussion.

Even an experienced talus hopper occasionally sends a block on its way. This awesome event, however, rarely causes panic, for the instant the boulder begins to roll, the expert is gliding toward an optional foothold that was routinely catalogued in the brain milliseconds earlier. The cry "Rock!" is airborne even before the new landing spot is reached. This instinctively shouted alarm informs hikers below to dart instantly toward a sheltered niche catalogued in *their* brains milliseconds earlier. Or else those below are purposely spread out far enough from the fall line to enjoy the ensuing rumbling dispassionately.

Such confidence does not come easily. How does the hiker learn to move adroitly down what Doug Robinson has called a "sea of holes"? How does he or she develop the leg strength necessary to absorb the cartilage-rending shocks received when moving efficiently down the obstacle course? Practicing talus walking is about as agreeable as practicing bivouacking, but beginners will have a more rewarding High Route experience if they endure a few hours of training. For the first lesson, choose a low-angled talus slope. Without a pack, work slowly down a hundred-yard course, then return and attempt the passage with more flair. Note that the feet stick to amazingly steep slabs if they remain there for only a fraction of a second. Notice how one teeters when moving slowly; appreciate how this potentially unsafe condition vanishes as the speed of descent increases. Finally, undertake the course with a pack, noting the disheartening loss of maneuverability. Once this gentle slope has been mastered, move on to a steeper incline to refine the techniques.

In time the novice will come to recognize the varying quality of footholds. For instance, small stones precariously balanced near the outer edges of talus blocks must be avoided at all costs. Similarly, sand or gravel that masks sloping holds presents an insidious hazard. The hiker soon learns that the smooth, flat surfaces of large boulders provide the most obvious and most secure holds. Other excellent holds can be found in the v-shaped slot where two or more boulders meet. Not only is the foot nicely supported in this gap, but if one boulder begins to shift, the hiker gains a precious extra moment to make the transition to another block. When the talus is wet or icy, this technique of using two adjoining rocks for stability proves especially valuable, for a wedged shoe cannot slip.

During the course of a talus scramble, the hiker's hands and arms contribute much more than might be expected.

On terrain made up of enormous blocks of granite, one weaves through labyrinthine corridors where the hands constantly brush the rock to maintain balance. But even on terrain where the rocks are three or four feet across, the hands play an important role. On steep talus the heel of the hand often acts as a braking mechanism as the crouching hiker descends a sloping boulder. A stiff arm can be used to bridge a gap, allowing the hiker to swing a leg to a lower hold. Cross-pressure techniques, where both arms —or both legs—span gaps to maintain balance, come into play constantly. Hikers who use all four limbs in an intelligent and fluid manner can flow down a steep slope without expending undue energy.

As mentioned earlier, the High Route does not traverse only endless slopes of talus. Rarely does the traveler struggle across these treacherous expanses for more than an hour at a time. Below the talus slopes, however, lurks another type of terrain that can cause problems for the beginner. Granite slabs are perhaps the single most aesthetic feature of timberline country, and they can be as easy to walk across as a sidewalk. But when they steepen —or display a scattering of sand—they can prove disconcertingly slippery. Fortunately, these slabs are rarely continuous, and the hiker who plans ahead can wander among them by means of the narrow ledges that so often interrupt them. If a slab must be climbed, remember to keep the weight directly over the feet. A hiker who leans into the rock, instinctively reaching for a handhold, will discover both feet oozing off the granite.

Small, hard-to-see irregularities in granite make excellent footholds, so always search out these blemishes. On smoother rock, plant the foot on the slab with the entire sole in contact with the rock, trusting that a few micro-crystals will keep the boot in place until the next one can be planted.

When descending steep slabs, resist the temptation to sit down and slide; this inelegant tactic will shred one's clothing as well as one's dignity. If the slab appears to be so steep and exposed that upright walking would be foolhardy, simply squat down and use flat-foot placements in conjunction with both palms. Moving one limb at a time, slowly shuffle downward. This stable posture should allow the hiker to descend all but the steepest slabs, the ones best left to confident rockclimbers.

High Route travelers who accomplish their journey in early season will encounter extensive snow, a far more treacherous medium than either talus or slabs. Numerous Sierra backpackers have been injured when they lost control on a steep snowfield and careened into the talus below. If the snow is rock hard—as it is early in the morning or in shaded couloirs—never venture onto it without an ice axe and a rope. Luckily, many High Route snowfields can be bypassed; those that can't should be attempted only in the afternoon, when the snow is softer and thus less slippery. Of course, not all snowfields are dangerous; low-angled ones with gradually tapering run-outs allow far easier walking than the trekker would find in the nearby talus. And, once in a great while, the experienced hiker will be able to enjoy glissading, that thrilling mountain activity akin to skiing without skis.

Stream crossings conclude this brief accounting of potentially hazardous terrain. Along the High Route these generally prove insignificant, for the traveler fords most creeks near their sources, where they are only a few feet wide. But there are exceptions, especially in the early season when the creeks churn tumultuously toward the lowlands. If a fallen log or a stream-spanning series of boulders cannot be located, one must wade. Here is the place to don a pair of lightweight camp shoes, for the rocks can be both angular and slippery. One person should scout a major crossing without a pack, first establishing that no rapids lurk just downstream. Unsteady hikers should have their packs transported across by the more confident ones.

Treading Softly in the Wilderness

As the High Route becomes increasingly popular, hikers will have to adopt certain preventive measures if the fragile landscape is to remain in the same condition as when the pioneers passed through it. Much of the potential damage to the timberline country—such as the creation of new trails, the pollution of water, and the degradation of campsites—can be prevented if travelers simply follow the few basic guidelines described below.

Faint paths are likely to evolve in such places as lake-shores, where each traveler tends to follow the same track. But in most of the High Route's meadowlands, the hiker can avoid creating even a semblance of a path by choosing a route that, by skirting the meadow, remains far from the delicate streamside. Similarly, when descending a sandy slope beneath a pass, the hiker should zigzag down the slope to the sides of the fall line to avoid creating an unsightly trench. Piles of rocks, called "ducks" or "stone men," also contribute to the establishment of new trails. Over a period of many years, well-intentioned hikers have built thousands of these markers to help subsequent travelers find their way over the rough sections of the High Sierra. The elaborately constructed monuments tend to channel hikers onto the exact same route, where a path soon develops. In all likelihood the ducked path is neither easier nor more direct than numerous alternate routes a few score feet distant; for this reason I recommend that High Route backpackers dismantle ducks wherever they are found.

In a region once famed for the purity of its water, the recent discovery of pollution in High Sierra streams seems particularly shocking. Every hiker suffers either directly or indirectly from this contamination, lending validity to the cliché about the absurdity of soiling one's own nest. In the past decade authorities have found such high levels of coliform bacteria—a sure indication of human feces—in certain streams that they recommend boiling the water from these streams for fifteen minutes, a laborious and fuel-wasting task. Serious diseases, some requiring lengthy and expensive medical treatment, can result from drinking contaminated water. This dangerous state of affairs will end only when *every* backpacker observes proper methods of wilderness sanitation. Two rules always must be followed when defecating: choose a site several hundred feet —or farther—from the nearest water; and bury the waste in a hole that can be covered completely. These measures should ensure that fecal matter will not be washed down into the water supply by rainwater.

Other diseases, not as serious, can result from the ingestion of soap; for this reason, perform all dishwashing chores and personal ablutions far from the banks of a stream or lake.

Much of the genuine physical despoilment of the mountain environment takes place in the vicinity of campsites. Popular places in the High Sierra show grievous damage from generations of campers. Bare-dirt patches indicate where hikers have set up their tents; flame-blackened boulders testify to once-roaring campfires; trash and human waste encroach upon campsites; and ancient pine snags, once beautiful, have been rendered ugly and desolate by seekers of wood. In popular locales where many such sites are clustered together, the drinking water is suspect, pack animals have churned the nearby meadows into fetid bogs, and hikers camp within a few feet of one another. The mere existence of these "slums"—occupied or not—means that an important aspect of the wilderness experience has vanished.

Fortunately, the above-described damage remains absent from most High Route campsites, and it must stay this way forever. For this reason, individual campsites are never mentioned in this guide, a departure from most guidebooks dealing with a specific mountain area. Instead of reading about campsites, the traveler will have to choose them in a more random fashion. This will not prove much of a hardship, however, for the High Route hiker is assured of discovering a comfortable spot almost anywhere in the flat areas near water below the 11,000-foot level in the southern half of the range, and below the 10,500-foot mark in the northern half. Numerous possibilities are apparent to anyone who studies the topo maps in advance; when finally arriving at a spot, it does not take long to find an ideal site. Hikers who choose locations never before used for camping will not only feel like pioneers; they also will have the satisfaction of leaving the site unsullied, an impossibility in an already damaged location.

To preserve the quality of these remote, pristine campsites—and to avoid further harm to already damaged ones —hikers should observe a few common-sense rules while traveling the High Route. A few suggestions are given below; rangers at Sierra roadheads also will have useful information.

Campsites always should be established as far as practical from any sources of drinking water; this preserves the quality of the water as well as saving the fragile streamside meadows from the inevitable trampling campsites receive.

Although the pioneers "rearranged" their camps to suit their needs, the present-day hiker should read about such practices, not emulate them. The day has long passed when the traveler can, with impunity, construct wind-breaks and tent platforms, or cut pine boughs for a bed.

Firewood has become so scarce in timberline country —and the remaining pine snags are so picturesque—that the camper should *never* build a campfire above the 9,000-foot level. If, for atavistic reasons, one occasionally must have a fire at lower altitudes, then use an existing fireplace and gather only downed wood. The modern gas stove is a marvelous, lightweight piece of equipment, and its use everywhere should be regarded as a badge of honor among High Route trekkers.

Needless to say, all garbage must be packed out of the high country; only a lazy or uninformed person buries cans and aluminum foil. Remnants of food *should* be buried; there is nothing less aesthetic than the sight of noodles reposing on a stream bottom like albino eels.

All of the above-mentioned guidelines lead to one axiom: do nothing to the landscape; simply walk gently through it by day and sleep lightly upon it by night. And, while doing so, imagine the thrill of returning some day to discover no visible change has taken place.

When To Go

Three phrases are used in this book to define the average seasonal conditions to be expected by High Route travelers. These phrases—*early season, midseason,* and *late season*—are by necessity arbitrary, depending as they do upon the previous winter's snowfall, the intensity of the spring's sunshine, and the pattern of autumn storms. For example, during the unusual drought of the mid-1970s, hikers wandered throughout the High Sierra, easily avoiding snowfields, as early as June 10. But during the summer of 1980 the snowpack, a less-than-average one, proved annoyingly slow to melt, with the result that as late as July 20 hikers had to slog across extensive snowfields.

Early season, as defined in this guide, encompasses the seven-week period from June 1 to July 20, a time when snow usually forms a dominant part of the Sierra scene. This snow can be rock hard in morning, and thus dangerous; it can be knee-deep by afternoon, and thus contribute to fatigue. Slopes and gullies on the north and east flanks of ridges can be blanketed by snow and ice, causing untold problems and dangers for hikers unaccustomed to such terrain. The weather can be unstable in early June, when minor storms often deposit several inches of fresh snow atop the melting snowpack. Crossing swollen streams proves tricky and even dangerous. Meadows, when not covered with snow, can be quagmires. There *are* advantages to traveling at this time of year: few hikers are encountered, mosquitoes are not yet aggressive, and gently sloped snowfields offer far easier traveling than the slabs or talus beneath. All in all, however, hikers without an experienced leader should plan on avoiding the High Route at this time of year because of the insidious dangers associated with snow.

Midseason, here defined as the six-week period from July 20 to Labor Day, traditionally has been the most popular time of year to visit the high country. The snow cover has disappeared, except in sheltered nooks. Wildflowers have burst forth in profusion, sometimes covering acres of meadowland. The weather remains so stable that the adage "it never rains at night in the Sierra" has some validity. Occasional afternoon thunderstorms contribute to the beauty of the range while simultaneously dissipating the haze created by forest fires. Mosquitoes have become a nuisance, but at least they have numerous victims from whom to choose, for the mountains are teeming with backpackers, especially on the established trails.

Late season, covering the interval from Labor Day to the first significant autumn snowfall, can be an excellent time to wander along the High Route. The crowds have returned to the cities, and the frigid night air has rendered the remaining mosquitoes apathetic. The summer haze has vanished, and from certain High Route passes it is possible to identify peaks ninety miles distant. The chief disadvantage of late-season travel concerns the uncertainty of the weather. A major storm often strikes the

Sierra Nevada during the first week of September. This tempest, sometimes displaying a brutal intensity (in 1978 such a storm killed three Sierra backpackers), deposits several inches of snow above the 10,000-foot level and ushers in the less predictable autumn climate. As this storm fades, the weather settles into an uneasy Indian summer, during which cold, clear spells can be interrupted by relatively benign intervals of rain and light snowfall. Since this snow melts quickly upon resumption of fine weather, it causes little trouble for the High Route traveler. Nevertheless, it should be obvious that those hikers who plan to venture into the high country after Labor Day must carry warm clothing and a storm-proof tent.

Late season gradually evolves into winter; by mid-November freshly fallen snow no longer melts, and the wind begins to howl incessantly. Only competent mountaineers familiar with alpine hazards have any business traveling the High Route for the next five months. By mid-April, when most of the avalanche danger has passed, the less rugged portions of the High Route will appeal to experienced cross-country skiers.

Safety Considerations

Unlike most of the other mountainous regions of North America, the High Sierra in summer is a gentle wilderness indeed. Absent are the shattered glaciers, killer storms, friable rock, and unpredictable grizzlies that make hiking and mountaineering in the Canadian Rockies, for instance, a far more dangerous proposition. Nevertheless, a few potentially serious hazards exist in the Sierra, and the High Route traveler should be forewarned.

Responsible leaders of High Route trips should make sure that all members of the party understand the consequences of an accident in the remote high country. A relatively minor accident such as a broken ankle not only will prove traumatic to the victim and spoil the trip for the others; it well may be an expensive mistake. As mountaineering accidents increase and rangers become overburdened in areas under federal jurisdiction, the authorities are considering billing injured persons for helicopter rescues.

Group members who wish to enjoy a safe trip should stick closely to their leader, never straying onto more difficult terrain. A hiker who feels threatened by the terrain at any point should speak out immediately; no one who realizes the consequences of an accident will think this a cowardly act.

Specific safety problems connected with loose talus, slippery slabs, steep snowfields, and stream crossings have been dealt with in the earlier section entitled "Rudiments of Cross-Country Travel." An additional hazard concerns mountaineering along the High Route. While the route itself involves absolutely no technical climbing—that is, ropes are not necessary—some of the most appealing nearby peaks are steep enough to require that the potential climber possess certain rockclimbing skills. Hikers un-trained in these skills often set out frivolously to reach such summits, and tragedy can result. Dangers lurk every-where on steep rock: handholds can break, the climber can slip off a scree-covered ledge, or the person can fall while negotiating an icy patch in a shaded gully. If the exposure is great enough, the fall can prove fatal. Attempting to ascend steep terrain without having gained experience on class 4 rock can only be called foolhardy.

Traveling solo along the High Route can be an enjoy-able, almost mystical experience. But all solo wanderers should leave their exact itineraries with both the rangers and a responsible friend, for even such a minor injury as a sprained ankle can have major consequences, especially in the off-season, when only a few people a week may be encountered along the route.

Hikers who travel in early or late season also should be aware of that insidious killer known as hypothermia. The typical scenario for death by "exposure" begins when an exhausted hiker pushes his or her limits during cold or windy weather. The first symptoms include an inability to keep warm, unusual weakness, and excessive grouchiness, soon followed by fits of uncontrollable shivering. When this shivering tapers off and finally ceases, death is immi-nent. All this can happen in the space of a few hours.

It is obvious that one must recognize this life-threaten-ing condition early in its subtle progress. Since the person who has hypothermia is usually the last to realize it, a competent leader should monitor all members of the party during cold or windy weather, watching especially for laggards who exhibit unusual behavior. A person who becomes thoroughly chilled, inexplicably tired, and uncharacteristically irritable probably has hypothermia. The party should stop immediately and set up a tent or windproof shelter. The victim should remove all clothes, slip into a sleeping bag, and be given hot drinks and high-energy food. If the hypothermia has progressed to the uncontrollable-shivering stage, another hiker should strip and get into the sleeping bag; the transfer of heat can effect a dramatic improvement in the condition of the chilled victim.

If hypothermia is treated during its early stages, the victim will be quite ready to travel the following day. In more serious cases, the person probably should be escorted from the high country as soon as possible.

Acute mountain sickness (AMS) can pose a problem to those High Route travelers who move quickly from sea level to 10,000 feet and above. Because less oxygen is available at high altitudes, the balance between water and electrolytes in the body is affected in ways not fully understood. Symptoms of the illness include headache, loss of appetite, nausea, and uneasy sleep. According to Dr. Charles Houston, an expert in the field of mountain sickness, the overall feeling is "very much like a bad hangover." Most persons will be fully protected from AMS if they take a full day to reach each successive 1,000 feet above the 7,000-foot level. Using this formula, one can see that at 13,000 feet the average person requires about one week to reach the point where strenuous exertion produces no ill effects. At this altitude, however, it takes at least one year before one acclimates fully and thus regains sea-level performance.

If the High Route traveler experiences AMS, there is only one practical solution, the same one recommended for hangovers: wait it out. Banish thoughts of climbing higher and drink copious quantities of liquid. A day of complete inactivity should alleviate most symptoms, although they could recur if the victim attempts to climb higher too quickly.

If time cures AMS, the opposite is true for another, far more consequential, form of altitude sickness. Death can come quickly to those unfortunates who suffer from high-altitude pulmonary edema (HAPE) and who remain at high altitude. Although extremely rare below 9,000 feet, the disease has struck numerous Sierra travelers at elevations not much higher. Symptoms of HAPE include severe shortness of breath, inexplicable weakness, and a cough that produces frothy, then bloody, sputum. The pulse rate is often high and vomiting may occur. Headaches may be violent or absent. A gurgling or bubbling sound emanating from the lungs is a frightening and unmistakable sign of HAPE. If someone is suspected of having this serious illness, transport him or her to a lower elevation *immediately,* even if this requires traveling at night or during a storm. A descent of even a few thousand feet often brings dramatic results, unless the disease has progressed too far. Meanwhile, rangers should be contacted and plans made for evacuation by helicopter.

Maps

The terrain covered by the High Route and its approaches is depicted superbly on eleven United States Geological Survey quadrangles. With a scale of 1:62,500 (approximately one inch to the mile), these fifteen-minute maps have proven remarkably accurate. The accompanying diagram indicates the names of the eleven maps and their geographic relationship to one another. Same-scale excerpts from these maps, covering the territory traversed by the High Route, have been included at the end of this book. (Since the High Route is not intended to be an actual trail, the course of the route has not been drawn onto these maps.) Thus, it is not necessary to purchase the U.S.G.S. quadrangles, though it should be kept in mind that the various approaches to—and departures from— the High Route rarely are shown in full on the excerpts because of their small size. Similarly, the complete quadrangles are needed in order to identify features lying more than a few miles from the route.

Quadrangle maps can be purchased in some sporting-goods stores near the Sierra, but backpacking specialty shops in major California cities usually offer a more com-

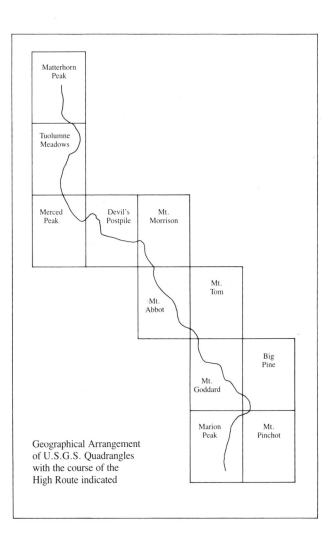

Matterhorn
Peak

Tuolumne
Meadows

Merced
Peak

Devil's
Postpile

Mt.
Morrison

Mt.
Abbot

Mt.
Tom

Mt.
Goddard

Big
Pine

Marion
Peak

Mt.
Pinchot

Geographical Arrangement
of U.S.G.S. Quadrangles
with the course of the
High Route indicated

plete selection. Hikers who plan their trip far enough ahead can be assured of obtaining all the maps they need by contacting the U.S.G.S. Branch Distribution Center, Box 25286, Federal Center, Denver, Colorado 80225. Request a current price list and a California order form.

Regulations

The Sierra Nevada, a relatively small range with more than twenty million people living within a day's drive, has experienced a population explosion in the past two decades. In August, dozens of backpackers cluster around the popular campsites deep in the mountains, and a continuous stream of hikers pass along the major trails. Although High Route trekkers rarely will encounter such scenes, they obviously still must obey the rules and regulations established by the U.S. Forest Service and the National Park Service in recent years to preserve the character of the wilderness. Most of these regulations are extremely sensible and easy to obey. For instance, one must camp at least 100 feet away from water whenever feasible, eschew wood fires in certain fragile areas, and avoid camping altogether in a very few overused sites.

Foremost in importance among the new regulations is one that requires every person entering the High Sierra to possess a wilderness permit. This rule enables the authorities to educate newcomers by plying them with literature when they pick up their free permits; the rangers also are able to limit the number of people who enter the high country on a given day. It is this latter restriction that can create potential problems for Sierra wanderers who plan to hike in midseason, the most popular time of year.

Requests for permission to travel in the High Sierra during this time of year should be made several months ahead of time if the traveler wishes to be guaranteed entry at a particular place and time. Fortunately, the rangers realize that not everyone can plan their trip far in advance, so they have set aside, at ranger stations near points of entry, a small number of permits available on a first-come, first-served basis. Thus, hikers who spontaneously plan a trip generally do not have to wait long for permission to enter the wilderness, especially if they are flexible enough to change plans at the last minute and choose another, less crowded entry point. Of course, backpackers who choose either the early or late season for their trips generally can avoid most of these complications.

A hiker who is caught without a permit will be assessed a hefty fine and ordered to leave the mountains; rangers regularly patrol the high country.

Listed below are the addresses and phone numbers of wilderness officials from whom advance permits can be obtained. A permit request should include the following information: date and place of entry; approximate day-today itinerary, with proposed campsites listed; date and place of exit; number in party; and number of pack animals to be taken (hopefully zero, since stock cannot be taken over most of the High Route).

- For entry at Kings Canyon, the southern terminus of the High Route, write to Kings Canyon National Park, Three Rivers, California 93262. Telephone: 209-565-3306.
- Those wishing to begin their trek at Bishop Pass, the gateway to the second leg of the route, should contact Inyo National Forest, 873 Main Street, Bishop, California 93514. Telephone: 714-873-4207.
- Hikers desiring to enter at Italy Pass, the approach to the third section of the High Route, should contact the Bishop office given above.
- For entry at Devil's Postpile, the start of the fourth segment, write to Inyo National Forest, Mammoth Lakes, California 93546. Telephone: 714-934-2505.
- Hikers heading north from Tuolumne Meadows over the final portion of the High Route should contact Tuolumne Meadows Visitor Center, Yosemite National Park, California 95389. Telephone: 209-372-4383.
- Backpackers desiring to work their way south from Twin Lakes, the northern terminus of the High Route, should contact Toiyabe National Forest, Bridgeport, California 93517. Telephone: 714-932-7070.

Place Names

Certain place names found in this guide do not appear on any official map, and the curious reader may wonder about their origins. Several of these names have been used in various guidebooks and have become fairly well known. Other names, bestowed decades ago, have faded into obscurity and are here resurrected. Some of the names are my own, invented especially for this book.

The following features were named by early Sierra pioneers and first appeared in print in the indicated annual issues of the *Sierra Club Bulletin:* Lake Frances (1905); Frozen Lake Pass (1923); Glacier Lake Pass (1938); Red Pass (1936); Snow-Tongue Pass (1905); White Pass (1936); and Windy Point (1936).

Guidebook writers often need to fabricate names in order to render complex terrain more understandable to their readers. The following features were named by unknown persons and initially appeared in print in the 1954 edition of *A Climber's Guide to the High Sierra,* published by the Sierra Club: Cirque Pass, Duck Pass, Feather Peak, Gabbot Pass, and Potluck Pass.

I invented the names Feather Pass and Horse Creek Pass for my 1976 version of the Sierra Club's revised guide, *The Climber's Guide to the High Sierra.*

Nancy Pass was named in the early 1970s by Don Scanlon in memory of his daughter; he affixed a plaque to a rock in the pass.

The name Vennacher Col first appears in the *High Sierra Hiking Guide to Mt. Pinchot,* published by Wilderness Press in 1974. The name Secret Lake appears in print for the first time in the same publisher's 1971 volume, *High Sierra Hiking Guide to Matterhorn Peak.*

The following names are solely my fabrications; applied mostly to passes, they either echo the name of an adjoining feature, commemorate some feature in proximity to a pass, or, as described in the text, refer to a significant historical event: Bear Lakes Basin, Bighorn Pass, Blue Lake Pass, Goat Crest Saddle, Grouse Lake Pass, Mine Shaft Pass, Puppet Pass, Shout-of-Relief Pass, Sky Pilot Col, Stanton Pass, Whitebark Pass, and White Bear Pass.

Rating System

Climbers long have used a rating system to differentiate the levels of difficulty encountered on a climb. Although such classifications rarely appear in this book, at times their use proves unavoidable. The following paragraphs briefly explain the system.

Class 1 indicates either trail walking or extremely easy cross-country travel. The class 2 category—common along the High Route—means that the terrain has become more rugged. At all times hikers must watch where they plant their boots; the hands must be used occasionally to maintain balance. Steep talus exemplifies this level of difficulty. Few hikers will have trouble on class 2 terrain.

Class 3 terrain is encountered on the northern side of a few High Route passes. Here, actual handholds and footholds must be found, tested, and used. The angle of the rock has steepened to the point where a fall might result in an injury. It is obvious that the traveler must use caution while moving across this type of terrain; inexperienced hikers should be aided in every possible way by persons more familiar with class 3 rock.

Class 4 terrain means that the holds have become smaller and the exposure has increased. A rope should be used to safeguard the climbers. In this book, only the ascent of Mount Humphreys falls into this category.

1

Early Exploration
of the High Sierra

THE REMARKABLE STORY of the pioneers who explored the timberline country of the High Sierra many decades ago remains relatively unknown today. Books such as Hal Roth's *Pathway in the Sky: The Story of the John Muir Trail* and Francis Farquhar's *History of the Sierra Nevada* deal briefly with these early explorations; but Roth's lavishly illustrated volume focuses, as its subtitle implies, on the history of the trail itself, and Farquhar's excellent work concentrates on the exploration—and subsequent development—of the periphery of the High Sierra, a story that encompasses such events as the discovery of Yosemite Valley and the influx of that frenetic group of gold-seekers known as the Forty-Niners.

The following history attempts to relate the story of the high-country exploration in a more comprehensive fashion than do the works cited above, for although the outlines of a story can be interesting, the details of the same story, seen in their proper context, can prove fascinating.

This account is admittedly biased in that it draws heavily upon the published recollections of those pioneers who were most committed to locating a "high mountain route" between Yosemite Valley and Kings Canyon. Although explorations of other significant regions of the High Sierra —such as the Mount Whitney massif—are mentioned herein for the sake of completeness, the emphasis has been placed on the wanderings that took place north of Kings Canyon, in that immense wilderness where the Sierra High Route traverses ridges and basins for nearly two hundred miles.

The articles and books written by the early explorers provide an exciting glimpse into an era when maps were either unavailable or inaccurate, trails were rudimentary, and travelers so few that when they encountered one another deep in the mountains, more often than not they would join forces for further exploration. These pioneers published dozens of lucid accounts of their journeys between 1863 and 1908, the most significant period of High Sierra exploration. After 1892, the year the Sierra Club was founded, many of these accounts appeared in that organization's well-respected journal, the *Sierra Club Bulletin.*

The men and women who described their travels during these years were educated and imaginative, eminently capable of capturing on paper the sense of wonder and euphoria they had experienced while tramping through the timberline country. But readers who peruse their accounts nowadays will be struck by a curious anomaly: sensitive though these writers were to their natural envi-

ronment, they failed to convey any of their emotions beyond the most simple and predictable ones, such as joy at
being in the mountains, or disappointment when stymied
by an obstacle. True, these explorers were, for the most
part, reserved, well-bred city-dwellers who kept their personal lives inviolable. And, of course, the forgiving atmosphere of High Sierra travel—compared, for instance, to
the stressful conditions found on an Arctic expedition—
meant that strong emotions probably rarely surfaced. Still,
if the early articles imply that such emotions as fear,
anger, and boredom were totally absent, perhaps present-
day readers can imagine, using their own trips as a basis,
the reality of the day-to-day life of the pioneers. Indeed,
one must conjure up these realities to avoid thinking of the
early explorers as sober demigods striding like robots
along preordained tracks.

The First Sierra Wanderers

Little is known about the high-country ramblings of the
first inhabitants of the Sierra Nevada, the Indians. Early
on, the indigenous peoples discovered they could safely
cross the highest parts of the range via several straightforward passes. The vast differences in ecology between the
moist, forested western slope of the Sierra and its desert-
like eastern flank meant that tribes such as the Miwoks
and the Yokuts, who lived on the western slope, coveted
the specialties of the main east-side tribe, the Paiutes, and

vice versa. Thus, using the high passes in summertime, the Indians living on the drier side of the range transported such goods as salt and pinyon-pine nuts westward, returning with, among other goods, beads made from seashells. Each tribe must have been astonished to find that the other would relinquish valuable commodities in exchange for common ones.

Whether or not the Indians ventured far from these trade routes remains unknown, but it is safe to assume that they rarely lingered in the timberline country. Living far below this region, rarely above the 4,000-foot level, the tribes of the western slope usually were assured of plentiful game and relatively benign winters. The natives living beneath the precipitous eastern flank undoubtedly avoided the ultimate heights because of the awesome topography. Nevertheless, during lean periods, both groups must have pursued their prey as far as timberline, and, if a wounded animal struggled higher, even toward the summits. Arrowheads have been discovered above 13,000 feet, but this cannot be construed as empirical evidence that the Indians themselves ventured that high, for a wounded deer could have floundered helplessly into the alpine zone, or later travelers could have transported the obsidian to these heights. Although the Indians must have reached minor summits and remote lake basins on occasion, it is likely that both hunters and tradesmen felt relieved when descending from that lonely, rocky world where the sun burned and the chill winds howled. The indigenous people, then, probably knew relatively little of the region now traversed by the High Route, for there was no compelling reason for them to explore such an unproductive landscape.

During the late eighteenth century and the first few decades of the nineteenth, the Spanish moved northward through California, establishing a string of twenty-one missions along the coastal region. They also settled in California's great central valley, and from this fertile plain they caught occasional glimpses of the high mountains to the east, bestowing upon them the prosaic name Sierra Nevada. Loosely translated, the name means a snowy, serrated range. While pursuing Indians, the Spanish made numerous forays into the foothills, but, satisfied that little of interest lay higher, they made no recorded attempt to reach the timberline country. Most of the largest rivers rushing from the heart of the range were named during the Spanish occupation, including the Merced, the San Joaquin, and the Kings. (The latter name is a shortened translation of the original—*El río de los Santos Reyes.*)

Lieutenant Frémont's Adventures

In the mid-1840s Lieutenant John Frémont of the United States Army was sent west with instructions to fill in certain gaps on maps of the American West. On his first trip—guided by Indians and accompanied by scout Kit Carson—Frémont crossed the Sierra Nevada south of

Lake Tahoe, discovering that marvelous body of water from the summit of a nearby peak.

On his second expedition, in 1845, the lieutenant surmounted the Sierra north of Lake Tahoe and descended the range's western flank to the great central valley. In mid-December Frémont, sixteen men, and a herd of cattle set off down the immense valley, intending to join the remainder of the expedition, which had been instructed earlier to cross the range far to the south. Failing to make the rendezvous, Frémont turned east toward the high mountains, hoping to encounter his compatriots. As the new year approached, the lieutenant found himself near timberline, burdened with cattle and ill-equipped for the biting cold. As if to cap the misery, snow began to fall. Abandoning their cattle, the men fled to the lowlands and safety.

Although the exact location reached by Frémont on his historic trip never will be known—his description is ambiguous—the easternmost point attained by the lieutenant must have been somewhere in the timberline country near the headwaters of the North Fork of the Kings River. Despite understandable worries about his men, Frémont seems to have enjoyed his brief sojourn, writing later that he had found the "exercise exhilarating."

Following the discovery of gold in the Sierra foothills a few years later, the vast hordes known as the Forty-Niners investigated every gulch and hillside in the Mother Lode country. Although the foothills thus were systematically explored, the miners paid scant attention to the less productive region high to the east.

The Surveyors

Even as late as 1860, ten years after California achieved statehood, little was known about the geography or resources of either the High Sierra or the other mountainous regions of the state. To rectify this situation the state legislature established the California Geological Survey that year. Soon called the Whitney Survey—after its leader, Josiah Whitney—this small band of professionals became the first to explore the timberline country officially. Since other areas of the state were deemed more important than the Sierra, it was not until 1863 that the group ventured into the heart of the range. Yosemite Valley, that spectacular glacial canyon linking the foothills to the high mountains, was relatively well known by the 1860s, and Whitney, William Brewer, and Charles Hoffmann spent eight days there, mapping and marveling. In late June the three men climbed northward out of the valley toward little-known territory. On June 24 they ascended a prominent peak that quickly was named Mount Hoffmann in honor of the group's cartographer. This straightforward climb marks the first verified ascent of a major High Sierra peak and symbolizes the beginning of an era that present-day mountaineers can only envy.

A few days later, from their camp near Tuolumne

Meadows, Brewer and Hoffmann climbed a massive peak on the main Sierra crest. So impressed were they with the view that Brewer persuaded Whitney to climb it with him the following day. According to Brewer's journal, Whitney "thought the view the grandest he had ever beheld, although he has seen nearly the whole of Europe."

This ascent of Mount Dana, easy though it was, marked the end of Josiah Whitney's mountaineering career. Perhaps he became altitude sick, perhaps he felt he could direct the Survey better from the big cities; in any case, he departed for the lowlands a few days later, never again to return to timberline country. William Brewer, at age thirty-four, became the de facto leader of the Sierra contingent of the California Geological Survey.

Brewer and Hoffmann, entranced with the high peaks surrounding them, soon set off to the south, following the Tuolumne River toward a looming, snow-clad mountain they had spied from Mount Dana. Since they had christened this latter peak in honor of the most prominent American geologist of that era, their next goal was named Mount Lyell, after the most eminent British geologist of the time. Although the glaciated mass proved "inaccessible," the two men at least were able to survey a large section of new territory.

During the journey toward Mount Lyell, the two men had discussed at length the course of the Civil War, finding parallels between that conflict and the insect world: "Mosquitoes swarmed in myriads, with not one-tenth the fear but with twice the ferocity of a southern Secessionist." Defenders of the Union, Brewer and Hoffmann had been distressed by the news received at their camp in Tuolumne Meadows: General Lee had invaded Pennsylvania with an army of 76,000 men. Not until a few weeks later did the climbers learn that the Battle of Gettysburg had been raging during the very hours they had spent just beneath Mount Lyell's summit, "at least sixty miles from civilization on either side, among the grandest chain of mountains in the United States."

The following year, 1864, marks the first recorded explorations into the unknown heartland of the central and southern portions of the High Sierra. Brewer, Hoffmann, Clarence King, James Gardiner, and several packers entered the mountains just south of the great canyon of the South Fork of the Kings River. In early July, Brewer and Hoffmann climbed a prominent, pyramidal peak; from the top of this 13,570-foot mountain the two men were captivated by the apparently endless array of spires, canyons, and cirques to the east. Taking advantage of the bird's-eye view, Brewer named many of the most prominent peaks, including one massive landform fourteen miles to the southeast: Mount Whitney. This mountain, they felt, was surely the range's loftiest point.

Back in camp, the two climbers of what soon was christened Mount Brewer related the day's adventures to the others. The vision of such high, unexplored peaks rising only a few miles away proved too much for Clarence King to bear silently. The twenty-two-year-old geologist, fresh from the Yale Scientific School, pleaded with Brewer to let him attempt one of the huge peaks, preferably Mount Whitney itself. Brewer had taken note of the chaotic landscape lying between Mount Brewer and the Mount Whitney massif; reluctantly, he gave his permission.

King and his companion, packer Richard Cotter, soon embarked on an adventure now part of High Sierra folklore. Their five-day trek across absolutely uncharted terrain involved the most difficult and intricate cross-country travel ever attempted in North America. The present-day backpacker who follows their general route will be quite impressed with the rugged and convoluted country in proximity to the serrated divide that separates the Kings and Kern rivers. Small cliffs continually block progress, and ledges that appear to lead to easier scrambling terminate over impassable dropoffs. Talus slopes prove to be steep and unstable, and treacherous snowfields linger throughout much of the summer. Nevertheless, the terrain that makes up the Kings-Kern Divide is by no means as intimidating as King implies in his embellished account recorded years later in *Mountaineering in the Sierra Nevada*. Most adventure writers of the late nineteenth century apparently felt their audiences would be impressed only with sensational feats, and the journey related by King consequently glows with drama and suspense. In one famous scene, Cotter, in the lead on a steep cliff, drops King a rope and informs him that he can place his weight on it if he so desires. Thus reassured, King decides it would be more sporting to climb the rock rather than the rope. Upon reaching Cotter, however, he is shocked to see his companion perched precariously on a sloping ledge. King realizes that they both could have fallen to their deaths had he actually tugged on the rope. Greatly impressed with his comrade's courage, King wrote that Cotter "might easily have cast loose that lasso and saved himself."

King's rendition of the ascent of their peak—not Mount Whitney, but by mistake the closer and lower Mount Tyndall—makes the reader wonder how both men survived. In spite of his embellishments, this journey must be regarded as the first truly ambitious cross-country undertaking in the High Sierra.

Later in July, a group of prospectors who had crossed the range from the east encountered Brewer's party and recommended a visit to the nearby gorge formed by the South Fork of the Kings River. Now world-famous as Kings Canyon, this idyllic valley served as the expedition's base camp for a week. In scouting the surrounding countryside, members of the Survey climbed north to the Monarch Divide, some 7,000 feet above the canyon floor. From this high ridge—the divide between the South and Middle forks of the Kings—the group bestowed the names of their two heroes, King and Cotter, on two conspicuous peaks to the east. To the north, far in the distance, lay a spectacular, jagged ridge of dark peaks: the Palisades

seemed an appropriate descriptive name. To the northwest, eighteen miles distant, rose an enormous, solitary
pyramid that the men named in honor of George Goddard, an early California surveyor. Present-day adventurers who travel the High Route will reach the approximate
spot from which these great peaks were named, and, later
on the journey, will pass so close to North Palisade and
Mount Goddard that their respective ascents will require
only a few hours' detour.

Unable to discover a pack-animal route over the Monarch Divide into the Middle Fork of the Kings, members
of the Survey instead ascended east up Bubb's Creek, a
major tributary of the South Fork. Following an old Indian trade route, the expedition crossed the crest of the
range at Kearsarge Pass and descended into the Owens
Valley, that vast trench lying below the eastern escarpment of the southern Sierra Nevada.

The expedition members quickly completed a fifty-mile
stretch up the Owens Valley and reentered the mountains
at Mono Pass, another ancient Indian route across the
range. From a camp on Mono Creek, some ten miles west
of the crest, Brewer, Hoffmann, Cotter, and a soldier
named Spratt attempted to reach lofty Mount Goddard,
then a few days' journey to the south. Cotter and Spratt
came within a few hundred feet of reaching the top, re-
treating only because both daylight and food were running
out. This epic trip, which traversed many miles of wild

and unknown country, merited just a few paragraphs in Brewer's journal; had Clarence King been along, the adventure surely would have formed an entire chapter in his book.

Brewer was becoming restless at Mono Creek, as his journal entry for August 14 indicates: "Rides over almost impassable ways, cold nights, clear skies, rocks, high summits, grand views, laborious days, and finally, short provisions—the same old story." Thus, on the following day the group began a hurried march toward civilization, reaching Yosemite a week later. The partial exploration of the Mono Divide marked the final High Sierra adventure for Brewer, who in a few months received a professorship at Yale, a position he was to hold for the next thirty-nine years. During his four years with the California Geological Survey, the scientist had traveled a remarkable 15,000 miles—half by horseback, 3,100 miles by foot, and the remainder by public conveyance.

Although the Survey was to remain active for another decade, its members rarely again ventured into the timberline country, and it is the expeditions of 1863 and 1864 that proved to be the most significant in the early history of the High Sierra. In 1865 a well-illustrated volume describing the Survey's work up to that time was published. This report, concerned mainly with the state's geology, nevertheless indicated the general course of the major Sierra rivers, informed the reader that prominent peaks had been named and charted, and related, in prose far less flamboyant than Clarence King's, that a few peaks now had cairns on their summits. One peak that remained untouched, however, was Mount Whitney, by 1865 acknowledged to be the range's highest summit. The travails endured by King as he pursued this goal form one of the most beguiling chapters in Sierra history.

Clarence King and Mount Whitney

King's failure to climb the great peak in July 1864 obviously had exasperated him, for immediately upon his return from Mount Tyndall he had begged his chief to let him try again. Brewer, knowing his assistant could fill in yet more blanks on the Survey's charts, gave the impatient youth a hundred dollars and an escort of two soldiers. This small expedition crossed the Kern River plateau and, after several days of needlessly complex maneuvering, finally set up camp beneath Mount Whitney. But King again failed to reach his goal, having inexplicably chosen the most difficult possible approach.

King's professional duties subsequently kept him in other regions of the United States until 1871, but in June of that year he detoured to Lone Pine, a village east of Mount Whitney, confident that he would not be rebuffed a third time. With a companion he managed to struggle upward to a prominent summit, but forbidding storm clouds blanketed the nearby peaks and rendered the view worthless. Although this meant that King could not confirm his success, he returned to his geological duties certain he had reached his goal at last. The word soon spread that the nation's highest peak had been conquered.

The emotions of the young geologist must have ranged from anger through disbelief to humiliation when, two years later, he read a scientific paper claiming that he had reached a "false Mount Whitney" in 1871. The person who had written this disturbing piece recently had ascended King's mountain (later to be named Mount Langley) and had been astonished to see, only five miles to the north, a significantly higher peak. King hurriedly entrained for California and on September 19, 1873, finally stood atop the towering peak he first had glimpsed nine years earlier. But there he endured yet another disappointment, for a note in a pile of rocks indicated he was not the first to reach the summit plateau. One month earlier, three men from the Owens Valley, hearing of the controversy, had taken advantage of their on-the-spot location to solve forever the mystery surrounding the mountain. And so ends King's final adventure in the High Sierra. As historian Francis Farquhar noted, King was "far too cock-sure, far too impetuous, to be a good mountaineer." Regardless of his ineptitude—or perhaps because of it—Clarence King remains one of the most endearing characters ever to roam the high country.

Prospectors, Adventurers, and Herders

Surveyors and miners were casual visitors to the High Sierra in the decades following King's misadventures. The Wheeler Survey, commissioned by the federal government, charted the rugged region north of Tuolumne Meadows during the late 1870s. Prospectors penetrated deep into the range, but, like the Indians, they preferred wooded valleys to alpine meadowlands. Only in a few locations did hardy miners ply their trade above timberline. Still, there can be little doubt that some of the summit cairns discovered by later travelers were constructed by these seekers of riches.

Other individuals curious to see or study the High Sierra also tramped through the range in the 1870s and 1880s, exploring new territory and making their findings public. The Kern River plateau, just west of Mount Whitney, was investigated by three men with the alliterative last names of Wales, Wallace, and Wright; their names now grace lakes in the vicinity. Judge E.C. Winchell of Fresno, California, spent several days in Kings Canyon, later penning a lengthy article for a San Francisco newspaper. The judge's son, Lilbourne, became, in 1879, the first person to stand atop Mount Goddard, the eminence that so dominates the central Sierra. Frank Dusy, a sheepherder, was apparently the first person to stroll along the floor of the immense gorge of Tehipite Valley, just a few miles north of Kings Canyon.

Most famous among the adventurers of this era was the naturalist John Muir. Arriving in the high country in the summer of 1868, the thirty-year-old Scot became an expert on the ecology of the High Sierra, formulating over a period of years his theory that glaciers were responsible for carving the U-shaped valleys so characteristic of the landscape. In addition to being a first-rate naturalist and writer, Muir was also a first-class climber. His ascent of Cathedral Peak in 1869 ranked as the most difficult climb yet accomplished in the United States. In the autumn of 1872 Muir guided a group of painters, including William Keith, to Tuolumne Meadows. Leaving his clients to work in this exceedingly lovely place, he set out alone toward the headwaters of the Middle Fork of the San Joaquin River. Lofty Mount Ritter was his goal, and he managed to reach its top successfully, though not without incident. Partway up a steep cliff, Muir found himself unable to move in any direction. Just as a fall seemed imminent, "life blazed forth again with preternatural clearness," and he was able to move gingerly upward.

Little is known about the exact course of Muir's wanderings, for though he kept meticulous and eloquent notes of the natural scene, he rarely reported his itinerary. At some point in his travels he is known to have climbed a high peak near the head of the South Fork of the San Joaquin River. He was under the impression he had climbed mighty Mount Humphreys, but historian Francis Farquhar, by matching Muir's description with known landmarks, believed it was far more likely that the naturalist had ascended Mount Darwin.

Of all the groups visiting the High Sierra during this era, none were so persistent as the sheepherders. The lush meadows sprinkled liberally throughout the western flank of the range—from the foothills to timberline—provided excellent summer forage for their flocks. Enormous numbers of sheep roamed the High Sierra during the second half of the nineteenth century, overgrazing the meadows and causing untold erosional damage. The sheepmen, naturally, were not concerned with the ecology of the Sierra; as soon as one meadow was devastated, the men would lead the "hoofed locusts"—as Muir called them—to another, more remote pasturage. In this manner the herders explored much of the timberline country, establishing crude trails in every region.

The American sheepherders of this time appropriated the vast meadowlands well below timberline; this usurption of the most desirable land meant that the Portuguese and French—the second-class shepherds—had to search elsewhere for pasturage. As a consequence, foreigners were the first to explore much of the highest countryside. In 1896, Theodore Solomons, the "father of the high mountain route," described the capabilities of these men: "The 'Portooge' can take his pack train, his mules or burros, over ground that baffles the mountaineering craft of the most experienced American herders, and the Frenchmen are said to show their heels to the Portuguese.

These Basques, or 'Bascoes' as they are called, who drive their sheep into the very teeth of the Californian Alps, are perhaps the most skilful mountaineers in the world." (Solomons surely would have altered this last sentence had he recalled the well-known exploits of English climbers such as Mummery and Whymper.) Even though there is no record of a herder reaching a difficult summit, it seems quite likely that some of the men occasionally scrambled up remote, rocky peaks in order to seek out the perfect meadow.

As city-bred mountaineers began investigating the High Sierra in the 1890s, they naturally sought out the nearest herder for advice about the lay of the land. "He is a good guide," Solomons once wrote, "but is nearly worthless in directing others. He will draw diagrams on the sooty bottom of the 'fry-pan,' which you must vow are lucid, though you know in your heart they are ridiculous. Moreover, the country immediately beyond the precise limits of his range is stranger to him than Afghanistan to a Bowery bootblack."

Heeding the advice of John Muir and the newly formed Sierra Club, the federal government began to oust sheepmen and their voracious flocks from national forests and parks, jurisdictions that by the 1890s covered much of the Sierra Nevada. Naturally, the herders resented this interference by outsiders. Detachments of cavalry eventually succeeded in ferreting the renegades out of the Yosemite high country. Many years later, after the destructive animals had been banished forever from the timberline country, mountaineer Chester Versteeg could write of this controversial era from a detached perspective: "Possibly, in our resentment at the manner in which the sheepman exploited the Sierra to his own ends, we are prone to forget the debt we owe him for preserving Indian routes and establishing new trails."

The Vision of Solomons

Few of the prospectors, adventurers, and sheepmen who roamed the Sierra during the last third of the nineteenth century displayed any enduring interest in the overall geography of the great mountain chain. Not since William Brewer's time had anyone seriously surveyed the central and southern portions of the Sierra. In the 1890s, however, a handful of curious adventurers independently decided to penetrate the range, discover its secrets, and announce the results to the world. The first of these pioneers to contemplate a major expedition into the unknown heart of the range was Theodore Seixas Solomons.

The boy of fourteen who gazed at the Sierra Nevada on a pristine spring day in 1884 was totally unaware that any human ever had set foot in the range. From his uncle's ranch near Fresno, young Solomons stared at the distant mountains, for the first time seeing them not merely as background objects, but as "the most beautiful and mysterious sight" he ever had beheld. The Holsteins grazing in the vast fields of alfalfa faded from the foreground, and he envisioned himself "in the immensity of that uplifted world, an atom moving along just below the white, crawling from one end to the other of that horizon of high enchantment." This account, written fifty-six years afterward, seems like a romanticized version of a youth's vision. Still, one would like to believe Solomons' claim that it was on this very day that he first imagined the "idea of a crest-parallel trail through the High Sierra."

It was not until 1892 that Solomons had enough money and time to set out on his quest for a high mountain route. With one companion, Sidney Peixotto, he journeyed to Lake Tahoe in mid-May. Their plan, Solomons wrote later, was "no less than the complete subjugation in a single season of the entire High Sierra." Even though the winter had been milder than usual, deep snowfields continually slowed the progress of the men and their two mules; they took six weeks to reach Yosemite Valley. There, by fortuitous coincidence, they encountered Joseph Nisbet LeConte, the twenty-two-year-old son of Joseph LeConte, the renowned geologist. (Twenty years earlier, the elder LeConte, along with John Muir, suggested that glaciation, not cataclysm, was responsible for canyons such as Yosemite Valley.) The younger LeConte, just beginning a distinguished career as a professor of engineering at the University of California, also was embarking on a series of trips—forty-four in all—into the highest and most remote sections of the range.

Solomons and Peixotto teamed up with LeConte for an excursion south toward Mount Ritter, that dark beacon that looms just south of the Yosemite National Park boundary. Following in the footsteps of John Muir, the three youths climbed the peak from the east; it was only the third time its 13,157-foot summit had been reached. Pleased with this conquest, the trio returned to Yosemite Valley.

By the beginning of August, Solomons felt the time had come to further "subjugate the High Sierra." But LeConte had business in the city, and Peixotto had doubts about continuing south. Perhaps the view from Mount Ritter's summit had discouraged Peixotto; perhaps he was weary after eighty straight days in the wilderness. It seems unlikely that the cause of his hesitancy was that he thought the "season was late," the polite excuse Solomons gave in 1940. It was, in fact, the ideal time to travel in the High Sierra. Whatever the real reason for Peixotto's defection, Solomons decided to push south with only a mule for company.

Heading south from Tuolumne Meadows along the same route he had traveled in late July, Solomons again climbed Mount Ritter, this time from the west. Fascinated by photography, the youth managed to transport a heavy and awkward 8 × 10 view camera all the way to the top, a feat that resulted in a set of alpine pictures that proved to be the first high-quality photographs ever taken of the High Sierra.

The wide, forested valley of the Middle Fork of the San Joaquin River beckoned next, so Solomons broke camp and headed downstream to Devil's Postpile, a geological curiosity previously known only to local miners and sheepmen. After skirting the southern ramparts of the Ritter Range, Solomons curved west, reaching civilization in early September.

During the course of his 1892 trip, Solomons either crossed or saw all three of the major forks of the San Joaquin River. He had camped at the headwaters of the Middle Fork; from Mount Ritter's summit he had gazed straight down upon the source of the North Fork. But of the South Fork—the High Sierra's longest river—he had obtained only an enticing glimpse. Solomons realized that this major watercourse likely sprang from a great cluster of peaks he had observed thirty miles to the south. The vision of this unexplored landscape haunted him for the two years that passed before he was able to return.

The 1894 expedition undertaken by Solomons and Leigh Bierce—son of author Ambrose Bierce—was something of a disappointment in that the two men failed in their principal objective: to reach the famed gorge of Kings Canyon via a route close to the Sierra crest. "Such a high mountain route," Solomons wrote in 1895, "practicable for animals, between the two greatest gorges in the Sierra, has never been found—nor, indeed, sought—so far as my researches have revealed." Yet the visionary was confident not only that such a route existed but that it "would be a journey fit for the gods." He further predicted that "as a scenic mountain tour, I doubt if the world affords its like."

Instead of heading directly for the South Fork of the San Joaquin River—their avowed goal—Solomons and Bierce lingered in Yosemite, exploring and photographing the high country. It was not until mid-September that the two men, along with three pack animals, began ascending the South Fork toward the Sierra crest. Warned by sheep-herders of the hazards accompanying autumn storms, the small expedition nevertheless worked far up the river, eventually curving east up Mono Creek, a major tributary. Soon the men reached a lovely valley, which Solomons named Vermilion Valley because of the color of its soil. Almost exactly thirty years earlier, William Brewer and his comrades had attempted Mount Goddard from this idyllic place. (In the mid-1950s the valley became Lake Thomas A. Edison, courtesy of the Southern California Edison Company.)

Solomons and Bierce next crossed into the Bear Creek watershed, following this turbulent stream first east, then south as it snaked toward its source. It was September 20 when they reached the base of an isolated peak that they christened Seven Gables because of its "eccentric shape." That afternoon the pair ascended the 13,075-foot mass and from its top stared in awe at the panorama. A multi-tude of peaks, mostly unclimbed and unnamed, rose in every quadrant. Immediately to the east lay a cluster of towering summits, below which nestled dozens of jewel-like lakes. The two men were quite probably the first humans ever to peer down into the wild set of cirques known today as the Bear Lakes Basin, one of the most striking landscapes traversed by the High Route.

Spectacular though the terrain was, Solomons knew they had reached an impasse, for their impending route, visible for the first time, looked feasible only to "mythological beasts with wings." Solomons soon conceived a bold plan: they would leave their pack animals with a sheepherder recently met downstream and set off south with fifty pounds each on their backs.

Before this plan could be effected, a major storm intervened, depositing several feet of snow. "We were on top of the Sierra," Solomons wrote, "some seventy-five miles of nearly waist-deep snow between us and the nearest settlements." It was obviously time for retreat. Unfortunately, the deep snow meant trail's end for the two remaining animals (the third had broken its leg and had been shot). One mule had strayed; it would either freeze or starve in the coming weeks. After shooting the other beast, the men hurried downstream. In the shambles of their camp lay the still-warm mule, their heavy camera, all the exposed negatives, and quantities of waterlogged bedding. Days passed as the exhausted pair retraced their route downstream; finally, on the fifth day, they stumbled upon a stranded herder who plied them with mutton. Their 1894 expedition came to an end shortly thereafter.

Apparently undeterred by this experience, Solomons returned the following year, this time with Ernest Bonner. (Solomons never traveled with the same person twice, a fact that may have several possible interpretations.) With fresh memories of the previous autumn, the obsessed twenty-five-year-old made sure to arrive in the mountains early. Ignoring Yosemite this time, the two men arrived at the site of the former camp below Seven Gables in late June 1895. During the following two weeks, while waiting for the snowpack to diminish, Solomons systematically explored the surrounding countryside, leaving Bonner to tend camp and their one pack animal. Exactly where Solomons wandered during this period never will be known, for his notes, donated to the Sierra Club library in San Francisco, were destroyed in the 1906 earthquake and fire. It seems likely that he would have ascended into nearby Bear Lakes Basin while searching for a passable route to the south; perhaps he even visited Feather Pass.

It is known that Solomons spent four days exploring the headwaters region of Mono Creek, and a photograph of the Mills Creek Lakes and Gabbot Pass, published in the May 1896 issue of *Overland Monthly,* indicates that he ascended Peak 12,691, a landmark on the ridge between the Second Recess and the Third Recess. (These great U-shaped valleys—there are four—were called "magnificent alpine recesses" by Solomons in his article; thus place names are born.)

Solomons was now, more than ever, aware that rugged

mountain travel could be accomplished far more effectively without pack animals. With this in mind, he and Bonner worked their way down to Jackass Meadow, on the South Fork of the San Joaquin River. There they left their mule with a sheepherder and, on July 12, began following the river south into new territory. The journey of the next two weeks ranks equally in Sierra history with the King-Cotter adventure of 1864. Solomons' accounts of this trip, published in various magazines and journals, are by no means as overblown as Kings'; indeed, his readable prose is eminently believable, and his enthusiasm for the High Sierra radiates from every page.

On July 14 the two explorers cached most of their equipment at the junction of the South Fork with the major tributary now known as Evolution Creek. Working their way up this stream, they soon emerged into an enchanting valley, where for three miles they strolled through pine forests interrupted by enormous meadows. Above what is now Evolution Valley—the "fairest paradise" Solomons ever had seen—the two men clambered up alongside innumerable cascades that raced down vast granite slabs. Reaching timberline at last, they beheld "a fine sheet of water," Evolution Lake. So impressed was Solomons with the magnificent scenery that he promptly bestowed names on nearly every peak in sight. These names, honoring philosophers and scientists prominent in the new field of evolution studies, included Mounts Darwin, Spencer, Huxley, and Fiske.

From their camp near Sapphire Lake, the two men climbed a prominent peak on the crest to the east. From the summit of Mount Wallace they could see that Mount Darwin was the region's highest peak; later that same day they made a bold dash for it, failing only a few hundred feet below the top when steep cliffs barred further progress.

On the following day Solomons and Bonner reluctantly departed the Evolution country, returned to their cache on the South Fork of the San Joaquin, and started south up the river. On July 19 they reached its source, the goal Solomons had been pursuing for three summers. Here, in an austere world of rock and snow, Solomons stood mesmerized by the looming black crags that surrounded him. Foremost among the peaks was Mount Goddard, the solitary monolith named by William Brewer's group thirty-one years earlier.

Solomons was not so vain as to imagine that he was the first person to stand in the shadow of the great peak. For one thing, he had seen evidence of sheep not far down the canyon. He knew, too, that Cotter and Spratt must have passed the headwaters on their 1864 attempt, and he realized John Muir had been somewhere in the area in 1873. Finally, Solomons was quite aware that Mount Goddard had been climbed in 1879 by Lil Winchell and Louis Davis. Nevertheless, it was a striking landscape, and Solomons must have been extremely pleased to have completed this segment of his dream route.

The next morning proved even more awe-inspiring, for the pair climbed the 13,568-foot Mount Goddard, obtaining the finest view they ever had seen in the Sierra. Virtually every major peak in the range, from Mount Conness to Mount Whitney—a distance of one hundred ten miles —was etched against the cobalt sky. Four hours passed as the two men absorbed the view, oblivious to an approaching storm. Rain poured down upon them as they stumbled down the steep talus. At 12,000 feet they reached the highest pines and stopped for the night. "We had no sooner built a fire," Solomons wrote later, "than the snow began to fall, and though for a time it was nip and tuck between the two elements, our pitch-saturated logs conquered at last."

In the dawn light the two men began traversing east through what is now the Ionian Basin. Their immediate goal was a pass Solomons had spied earlier from the vicinity of Evolution Lake. If they could reach this broad saddle—now called Muir Pass—Solomons felt certain they could then descend into the headwaters region of the Middle Fork of the Kings River. But the storm's intensity increased, thwarting these plans. After struggling across slippery talus for several hours, Solomons resolved to flee the inhospitable alpine world and drop south into a deep gorge he had noticed from Mount Goddard's summit. Passing between two guardian peaks—immediately named Scylla and Charybdis—the adventurers began their descent. Acres of enormous boulders blocked the canyon floor, making their progress painfully tedious. In the rain, the slate forming the canyon walls shone like lustrous metallic plates. This narrow canyon—both sinister and beautiful—was named the Enchanted Gorge. (So remote is this feature that only three more parties were to pass through it during the next half-century.)

It was midafternoon on the following day when Solomons and Bonner emerged from the confining canyon into the flat meadowlands bordering the Middle Fork of the Kings River, having made a bone-jarring descent of 7,600 feet in just two days. They had crossed the divide separating the San Joaquin watershed from the Kings drainage by just about the most difficult possible route. The remainder of the trip from Simpson Meadow, on the Middle Fork, to Kings Canyon, on the South Fork, was anticlimactic, for a well-established trail led across the Monarch Divide.

Solomons realized that pack animals could not be taken through the Enchanted Gorge, and since his ambition always had been to discover a crest-parallel route negotiable to stock, he was back in the mountains the following summer. His companions in 1896 were two students from the University of California: Walter Starr and Allen Chickering. The three men, along with four horses, left Yosemite Valley on July 3. In mid-July, however, Solomons became ill and decided to leave the expedition near Jackass Meadow. The other two men, evidently not as obsessed as Solomons with a *high* mountain route, continued south through the forested country far to the west of Mount Goddard. Reaching Kings Canyon on August 3, the pair became the first ever to travel with pack animals from Yosemite to Kings Canyon. Although this was a praiseworthy accomplishment, they had traveled almost exclusively in the lowlands, far from the Sierra crest.

Theodore Solomons was not destined to return to the watershed of the Kings River. Perhaps he finally became discouraged with furthering his high mountain route; in his later writings he does not mention his reasons for abandoning his quest when it was but halfway accomplished. In 1897, instead of pushing south into the Kings River headwaters, as one might have expected, he "made improvements in the northern part of the route." It is possible that only the San Joaquin drainage truly fascinated him; certainly his name will be linked forever to this immense wilderness. During his five journeys between 1892 and 1897, Solomons bestowed approximately 150 place names, about 60 of which remain today. A short time after these Sierra trips, he moved to Alaska, revisiting the San Joaquin region only once again, in 1932. In 1933 he wrote that he had departed from the Sierra in 1897 assured about the completion of his high mountain route: "As for the Kings River section . . . I knew that with LeConte, Bolton Coit Brown and one or two other indefatigable ones, it was in safe hands."

Bolton Coit Brown and the Kings Watershed

If Solomons had been obsessed with the San Joaquin drainage, Bolton Coit Brown surely was convinced that the Kings River watershed afforded the finest Sierra adventures. A professor of fine arts at Stanford University, Brown made three memorable visits to this area between 1895 and 1899. Unlike Solomons, he displayed little interest in a continuous Sierra high route, preferring instead to concentrate his energies in just one region. Using Kings Canyon and nearby Paradise Valley as his chief base camps, Brown thoroughly investigated the rugged country surrounding the headwaters of the South Fork of the Kings River.

The professor's 1895 trip to Arrow Peak remains a classic of solo exploration. Leaving Kings Canyon with one mule in late July, Brown trudged up the well-worn path leading over the Monarch Divide toward the Middle Fork. It seems entirely possible that along the way he encountered Solomons and Bonner, enervated from their descent of the Enchanted Gorge. If this meeting took place—both Brown and Solomons independently write of traveling this segment in late July—no record exists. But one can almost picture the trailside conversation. Solomons, intensely pleased with his pioneering efforts, well may have crowed a bit as he bestowed advice on newcomer Brown. Ironically, Solomons could not have known he was completing his last significant High Sierra exploration as he spoke to his unknowing heir for the first and perhaps last time.

After spending a few days exploring the great canyon of the Middle Fork of the Kings, Brown began working up Cartridge Creek. This major tributary of the Kings climbs steeply east toward Cirque Crest, a northeasterly extension of the Monarch Divide. Leaving the heavily forested valley behind, the professor and his mule reached timberline country near Marion Lake. Shortly after passing this pleasant body of water, Brown was astonished to see a human bounding down the hillside. It was a French sheepherder, complete with dog and flock; the man indicated to Brown that the wide gap just to the south was passable to stock.

On the following morning Brown ascended to what is now Cartridge Pass. Scrambling from the saddle up to the summit of nearby Mount Ruskin, the professor looked straight down into Upper Basin, the source of the South Fork of the Kings River. He counted twenty-six sparkling lakes scattered over hundreds of square miles of pristine wilderness. To the east, across Upper Basin, rose the impressive ramparts comprising the crest of the Sierra. Among these peaks was one with a conspicuous gap on its broad summit; Brown named it Split Mountain. A striking symmetrical peak to the south was christened Arrow Peak. (A short time later, the professor wrote an essay dealing with the naming of mountains. In it he chastises Theodore Solomons indirectly by decrying persons who name mountains in honor of people, especially "men eminent in the physical sciences." Names such as Bridal Veil and Devil's Slide also earned his ire: "All such pseudoromantic appellations smack of childishness and of cheap sentimentalism.")

From his camp on the South Fork of the Kings River, Brown stared with uncertain emotions at the classically shaped ridges rising to the summit of the newly named Arrow Peak. The professor was in a quandary. He was low on food, and his shoes were in tatters; he obviously should return as soon as possible to Kings Canyon. Yet, he wrote later, the peak "called to me at breakfast, its rocky pinnacles beckoned me, its soaring summit challenged me. I could stand it no longer and hurriedly swallowing the last of my coffee, I threw prudence to the winds . . . and was away through the pines and the boulders, over the roaring stream . . . almost on the run for the sheer joy of that mountain. . . ." Possessing such a positive attitude, he was, of course, successful; from the summit his artist's eye spotted thirty-two lakes.

During the next few days Brown worked his way down the South Fork, knowing it would take him directly into Kings Canyon. But the terrain was rough, with brush and talus denying easy progress. At last Brown's mule became lame and could go no farther. Shouldering an enormous pack, the professor set off down the wild, white-walled canyon known today as the Muro Blanco. A few days later he returned to civilization, "shockingly ragged and sun-burned and dusty."

In the summer of 1896 Brown and his bride, Lucy, spent a month and a half exploring the Bubbs Creek watershed and the region to its south. After climbing for several weeks in the environs of Bullfrog Lake, the honeymooners crossed the Kings-Kern Divide at an obvious low point near the notch negotiated thirty-two years earlier by Clarence King and Richard Cotter. Brown was quite likely the first person to speculate in print about the accuracy of King's account: "I am strongly inclined to suspect that there was a general tendency with Mr. King to put down the things he did not himself do as impossible. His book is very far from giving a true impression of the region from Brewer to Tyndall."

Lucy Brown proved to be as tough a mountaineer as her husband, judging from the following one-day exploit. Arising from a wet bivouac, where they had dozed fitfully, the pair left their timberline camp at the headwaters of the Kern River and headed east, intending to try Mount Williamson. Not knowing its exact location, they mistakenly started up a spur of the Kings-Kern Divide. Soon the couple recognized Williamson, some five miles to the east. They abandoned the spur, sped across the tundra of Tyndall Creek Basin, and by noon stood atop California's second-highest peak. Retracing their steps nearly to their bivouac site, the Browns then turned north, crossed Harrison Pass at sunset, and stumbled down 3,500 feet to their main camp at East Lake. During this fifteen-hour odyssey, the professor and his wife had tramped across twenty miles of rough cross-country terrain, coped with an elevation gain of 5,000 feet, and descended approximately 7,000 feet. The next day the newlyweds easily managed the fourteen-mile jaunt back to Kings Canyon.

Later in the summer of 1896 Brown managed yet another remarkable feat, this one alone. A year earlier he had attempted the unclimbed Mount Clarence King, failing only a few hundred feet below the summit. Now he was anxious to try the striking horn of granite once again. During the course of one long day, Brown made the first ascent of the peak from his camp in Paradise Valley. But it is neither the elevation gain of 6,300 feet nor the distance of twelve miles that is especially noteworthy. What makes this ascent so significant is the difficulty of the upper few hundred feet, for the summit region, composed of gigantic blocks and slabs, is sheer on some facets and merely steep on the others. Brown carefully squirmed up intricate passages until finally, a hundred feet below the top, he came to an apparent impasse. Tying a knot in the end of a piece of rope, the professor cast it upward repeatedly until the knot lodged in a crack. Using the rope for assistance, he inched higher. He performed this clever and unusual technique several more times before reaching "the ugliest place of all," the summit block itself. There he tossed a short loop of rope over a rounded projection just above his head and slowly shifted his weight onto the loop. It held, and he levered onto the summit, completing the most difficult North American rock climb of the nineteenth century. (Today his route is rated 5.4, meaning that ropes and protection should be used.) The view was spectacular and the exposure frightening. Imagining the consequences of a slip, Brown later wrote in the same vein as the man for whom the peak was named: "If you fall off one side, you will be killed in the vicinity; if you fall off any of the other sides, you will be pulverized in the remote nadir beneath."

Three years went by before Brown returned to the Kings River drainage. This time he was accompanied not only by Lucy, but by their two-year-old, Eleanor. The family spent most of their vacation investigating the beautiful lake basins just east of Mount Clarence King. At some juncture, Brown relaxed his strictures on never naming features after people, for the largest Rae Lake appears on his published map as Lake Lucy and its most prominent isle as Eleanor's Island. Oddly enough, however, not one of the place names the professor bestowed in this area ever became official, in marked contrast to the features christened by Theodore Solomons.

Following his trip of 1899, Brown seems to have abandoned the High Sierra. His well-written articles, so prominent in the early issues of the *Sierra Club Bulletin,* ceased in 1901.

LeConte, the Chronicler

The late 1890s mark the emergence of yet another noted Sierra explorer, Joseph Nisbet LeConte, whose informative articles, maps, and photographs were to grace the *Bulletin* regularly for the next forty years. (For the remainder of this book, the name LeConte, unless otherwise stated, refers to this adventurer—not his father, also Joseph.)

As mentioned earlier, LeConte had accompanied Theodore Solomons and Sidney Peixotto on a trip to Mount Ritter's summit in 1892. During the next few years, the diminutive LeConte journeyed to the High Sierra several more times, concentrating his efforts in two locales: Yosemite National Park and the Kings Canyon area. In the course of these adventures, the young professor created a set of photographs so excellent that in 1944 Ansel Adams was to praise their quality and aesthetic values: "His photographs are not the fruit of intellectual cogitations; they are the natural, inevitable selections of a man very much in tune with the world about him. . . ."

Early on, LeConte also became fascinated with the idea of mapping the high country, and to this end he obtained information from Solomons, Brown, and others, in addition to acquiring firsthand data. In 1893 the Sierra Club published his initial efforts—maps of the Yosemite and Kings Canyon regions. These maps, revised at intervals as new information became available, were greatly appreciated by the members of the newly established mountaineering and conservation organization; this reception unquestionably spurred LeConte to broaden his knowledge of the range.

LeConte's first significant mountaineering venture outside his familiar haunts—Yosemite and the Kings Canyon region—came in 1898, when he and Clarence Cory decided to explore the possibility of a true high mountain route between these two locales. During the early part of their month-long journey, the two men closely followed the pioneering route of their predecessor, Theodore Solomons, even to the extent of visiting the upper reaches of Mono Creek. From a camp near the junction of this stream and the Second Recess, the pair made the first ascent of Red Slate Mountain, the towering sentinel of this part of the Sierra. A few days later, from the top of Seven Gables, they were awe-struck by the sight of unclimbed Mount Humphreys, a solitary monolith nine miles to the east. At that moment the men resolved to try for its tapered summit.

LeConte and Cory attempted to lead their pack animals toward the huge peak; finding no practical route, they returned to Blaney Meadows, a lush parkland on the South Fork of the San Joaquin River. Leaving their stock behind, the pair knapsacked into Humphreys Basin, a wild and austere region dotted with dozens of rockbound lakes. On July 7 they made their bid for the summit. After several false starts on various ridges, the men finally reached a small prominence on the mountain's northwest ridge, 500 feet below the top. The view upward was discouraging, as evidenced by LeConte's later description: "I have never felt so impressed, so utterly overpowered, by the presence of a great mountain as when standing amongst the crags of Mt. Humphreys looking up that smooth wall to its airy summit, and again down ten thousand feet into the depths of the Owen's Valley." So intimidated were the two men that they fled down the mountainside without even attempting the summit pinnacle. The immense landmark of the central Sierra would remain unascended for a few more years.

Kings Canyon beckoned, so the two young men returned to their pack animals and began ascending toward the source of the South Fork of the San Joaquin. But upon climbing Mount Goddard they suffered a major disappointment, for they saw that it was impossible to lead their stock across the rugged divide anywhere near the great peak. Luckily, they recalled that sheepherders earlier had mentioned a pack-animal route that circumvented the divide by means of the basins at the headwaters of the North Fork of the Kings River, only a few miles to the west. Back down the San Joaquin the two men went, searching for a way across the ridge known today as the LeConte Divide. Discovering a passable route at last, the expedition soon reached the forested country visited by John Frémont and his men a half-century earlier.

A week later LeConte and Cory attained their goal,

thus accomplishing the second complete journey between Yosemite and Kings Canyon. For a short distance they had traveled closer to the main crest than had their predecessors, Starr and Chickering; nevertheless, no one yet had traversed the southern Sierra close to the headwaters of the Middle and South forks of the Kings River. The six-mile-long barrier known as the Goddard Divide, stretching from the LeConte Divide to the main crest, had forced all travelers into the less rugged country to the west. LeConte was to experiment with this crossing again, but not immediately, for he long had been fascinated by distant views of the Palisades, that serrated ridge named by Brewer's survey group. The next few summers, he decided, would prove rewarding if spent in this remote region.

As his first goal, LeConte chose the massive southern outrider of the Palisades, Split Mountain. Traveling the by-now familiar route from Kings Canyon, across the Monarch Divide, to the Middle Fork of the Kings, LeConte and his wife camped at lovely Simpson Meadow for a few days, savoring the scenery and the trout. On July 18, 1902, the couple and Curtis Lindley ascended alongside the Middle Fork until reaching Cartridge Creek; from this confluence they followed Bolton Coit Brown's 1895 route to Marion Lake—named on this 1902 trip by LeConte in honor of his wife of one year, Helen Marion Gompertz LeConte.

From the vicinity of Marion Lake the trio explored

potential routes across the notched ridge separating them from Upper Basin, the source of the South Fork of the Kings. None of the notches reached on July 23 proved passable on their eastern sides, but on the following morning the undaunted threesome shouldered their packs and set off to reconnoiter the passes missed the previous day. Just when the venture seemed doomed, LeConte discovered what is now called Frozen Lake Pass, "the only point where the Cartridge Creek Divide can be crossed." Beyond the 12,400-foot saddle lay Upper Basin, covered with tarns and tundra.

The next morning's climb of Split Mountain was somewhat anticlimactic, for the mountain proved to be one of the easiest LeConte ever had climbed. As usual, though, the view was spectacular, and he marveled at the complexity of the terrain: "For eighteen miles to the south, and eighteen miles to the north not a single one of the countless giants of the Main Crest has ever been climbed. We were in the heart of the High Sierra." The Palisades loomed to the northwest, but LeConte realized that their provisions had nearly run out; the dark cluster of summits so dominating the skyline would remain untouched for the time being. From their camp at Marion Lake, however, LeConte and Lindley dashed to the north to reach a mountain appropriately christened Observation Peak. From this vantage point the highest crags of the Palisades rose in full view, only five miles distant. LeConte mapped the area as best he could and vowed to return the following year.

Although the Palisades remained the last major uncharted region of the High Sierra, LeConte knew that the periphery of the group had been explored by sheepherders and prospectors. Bishop Pass, immediately north of the highest summits, was a known sheep route across the Sierra crest. Dusy Basin, that intriguing mélange of water, stone, and pine just west of the pass, had been investigated in 1877 by Frank Dusy, a peripatetic sheepherder. Two years later, Lil Winchell, on his journey toward unclimbed Mount Goddard, passed close enough to the Palisades to name two of them. Later still, Theodore Solomons had viewed the jagged peaks from the top of Mount Goddard; some time after, in an article for *Overland Monthly,* he lavished excessive praise on the group: "The Palisade country, I have reason to believe, is the acme of alpine sublimity on the American continent." Of the jutting peaks themselves, however, absolutely nothing was known except their outlines and approximate elevation, 14,000 feet.

LeConte was determined to investigate the Palisades at closer range, so in July 1903, James Hutchinson, James Moffitt, John Pike, Robert Pike, and the two LeContes retraced the previous year's route as far as Marion Lake. Leaving Helen LeConte and John Pike to tend camp, the four others struck north. Skirting Observation Peak on its east flank, the group dropped nearly 3,000 feet to an idyllic glade at the 8,800-foot level of Palisade Creek. This place, according to LeConte, was "absolutely untouched. Not since the creation of the forest reserve [in 1893] had human foot trod this glorious wilderness, and even before that time the sheepmen who visited the valley must have been few indeed, for not a blaze, monument, nor corral did we see, and there were but few signs of old sheep-camps."

That night's camp was established at timberline on Glacier Creek, not far below the mysterious peaks. Early on July 24 the men left camp and continued up the stream, traversing meadows, talus, and finally snowfields. Here they encountered acres of sun cups, a phenomenon familiar to all who venture into the subalpine world. LeConte described them succinctly: "The unequal melting of the snow cut the whole mass up into a labyrinth of great knife-blades, which were sometimes four feet high and two or three feet apart. We were forced to step from blade to blade, balancing on the sharp edges, and often falling into the spaces between."

In spite of these obstacles, the well-conditioned men soon reached the main Sierra crest, astonished to see, just below them, what they knew must be the largest glacier in the range, complete with crevasses and a mile-long bergschrund. Greatly impressed with this unexpected sight, they turned toward the highest peak—North Palisade—and gasped. The jagged, half-mile ridge leading over to its summit appeared impossible. Hutchinson carefully traversed to the brink of a huge gash—now called the U-Notch—and verified the prognosis. The disappointed men scrambled up a consolation prize to the east—Mount Sill, a massive peak that LeConte had seen, and named, seven years earlier. To LeConte, the view from this 14,162-foot summit was "unparalleled in grandeur and extent." But there was no question in anyone's mind that the view was flawed in one respect: the image of nearby North Palisade, eighty feet higher and still virgin.

The next morning, unwilling to abandon their primary objective without at least one serious effort, LeConte, Hutchinson, and Moffitt set off from camp once again. From what is now Potluck Pass—reached by the present High Route—they gained an excellent view of North Palisade's 1,500-foot-high southwest face, an imposing escarpment riven only by a few steep chutes. Choosing the most prominent of these, the three climbers worked up it until stymied by steepening cliffs. Since these appeared unclimbable, it seemed the group must fail once again. But as LeConte peered down the chute they had just ascended, he spied a narrow ledge snaking around a corner. This proved to be the key to the ascent, for the sloping shelf led to an easier chute, which eventually ended near the summit. The highest of the Palisades had been vanquished, and the geography of yet another remote part of the High Sierra was better understood.

With the three highest summits of the Palisades conquered, LeConte returned to the Evolution country during the summer of 1904, accompanied this time by the eminent geologist Grove Karl Gilbert. The object of their journey—to travel from Yosemite to Kings Canyon as close to the Sierra crest as possible—was identical to that of LeConte's trip of 1898. But this time LeConte vowed to find a route for animals across the Goddard Divide.

On July 18, while sixty-one-year-old Gilbert studied the rocks of the Evolution Lake region, LeConte followed Evolution Creek as it curved toward its source. The terrain proved remarkably gentle as far as the top of the Goddard Divide, but there, at what is the present-day Muir Pass, he stared down in dismay at "the savage black gorges of the Middle Fork region." This sobering sight convinced LeConte that stock could not be taken across the divide; furthermore, he saw no signs of sheep, another indication of the terrain's roughness. A few days later the discouraged men tramped west and crossed the LeConte Divide at a notch just south of the one crossed by LeConte and Cory six years earlier. The new notch became Hell-for-Sure Pass, surely one of the most evocative place names in the High Sierra. A week later the expedition reached Kings Canyon, their fine trip marred only by their failure to cross the Goddard Divide.

Hutchinson, the Mountaineer

James Hutchinson, pleased with his ascents in the Palisades the previous year, was active also during the summer of 1904. The San Francisco attorney was the preeminent climber of the Sierra during the early years of this century, complementing his friend LeConte, who was unquestionably the range's most prominent explorer, mapmaker, and photographer. With his brother Edward and two other men, Hutchinson entered the mountains in mid-July with a bold goal in mind: the ascent of the still unclimbed Mount Humphreys.

At Blaney Meadows the group encountered Gilbert and LeConte, the latter welcoming his Bay Area friends and begging to hear the news from home. "All the afternoon," LeConte wrote in his diary, "I talked with my friends, and smoked their cigars and drank their benedictine." The two parties traveled together as far as Colby Meadow, that exquisite spot at the head of Evolution Valley. (Readers familiar with Sierra geography may wonder why Hutchinson ignored Piute Creek, a far more direct route to Mount Humphreys. Lacking lightweight food and equipment, early travelers depended greatly on pack animals to transport their necessities; Piute Creek, extremely rugged in its lower reaches, was not feasible for stock.)

Leaving LeConte and Gilbert to their explorations of the Goddard Divide, Hutchinson's group ascended a faint sheep path leading up the north wall of Evolution Valley. Soon they arrived at a superb campsite, a lake "fringed with the exquisite alpine heather," as Hutchinson later wrote. In the background loomed a multitude of unclimbed peaks; closer at hand the men were amused by the antics of dozens of gray-crowned rosy finches, those hyperactive denizens of the subalpine zone. The beautiful lake, situated on a high bench overlooking Evolution Valley, was named Lake Frances, after one man's wife. It was to lose this name in later years, appearing on the map simply as Lake 11,106.

A reconnaissance by two of the men to the top of the nearby Glacier Divide—which they would have to cross to reach Mount Humphreys—provided a dramatic view of their goal, only four miles to the north. But the foreground terrain worried the men, for steep cliffs and ominous couloirs on the north side of the ridge looked difficult for humans and certainly impassable for stock. On the following day, having tethered their mules to shrubs along the shoreline of Lake Frances, the men were able, with only a few moments of apprehension, to cross the divide at what immediately was dubbed Snow-Tongue Pass. Four tired mountaineers set up camp that night in desolate Humphreys Basin.

At dawn on July 18 the quartet set off toward one of the range's most spectacular summits. Wary of facing the difficulties of the route attempted by LeConte and Cory, Hutchinson led his team up a different side of the mountain. Sheer cliffs blocked the upper part of this route also, but the confident Hutchinson made a courageous—or perhaps foolhardy—effort and succeeded in surmounting a frightfully exposed wall. Edward Hutchinson managed to struggle up a rope cast down by his brother, but their two companions demurred, contenting themselves with the ascent of a nearby pile of rocks they facetiously named Married Men's Point. A few minutes later, at precisely the moment Joseph LeConte strode alone onto the barren saddle of Muir Pass, the Hutchinson brothers clambered onto the exposed summit rocks of 13,986-foot Mount Humphreys. Another Sierra giant had fallen.

Sierra Club Outings

LeConte and Hutchinson were hardly the only wanderers in the High Sierra during the early years of the twentieth century. Although these two men were certainly the most ambitious and skillful mountaineers of this era, many fishermen and hikers also tramped through the mountains, investigating remote cirques and following streams to their sources. These pioneers occasionally published accounts of their journeys in such popular magazines as *Sunset* and *Overland Monthly.*

During this same period, participants in the soon-to-be-famous Sierra Club outings began to publish articles in the *Sierra Club Bulletin,* thus conveying a vast body of information to other Club members and the general public. The inspiration for the first of these outings came to William Colby in 1900. Upon learning of an Oregon club's recent summer trips to the Cascade Range, the twenty-five-year-old mining engineer approached the directors of the Sierra Club with a proposal for a Club-sponsored trip to Yosemite National Park. With the enthusiastic support of the organization's president, John Muir, Colby had little trouble convincing the hierarchy that his plan was feasible. Thus, in mid-July 1901, ninety-six Club members gathered in Yosemite Valley, the staging area for the journey toward their main camp at Tuolumne Meadows. Included in this group were Muir, his daughters Wanda and Helen, the noted landscape artist William Keith, and the chief of the United States Biological Survey, C. Hart Merriam. (Each of these five pioneers has since been honored by at least one Sierra place name.) Excited to be embarking on an adventure into the unknown, the trip participants nonetheless were saddened to learn that one of their most venerated members would not make the journey: renowned geologist Joseph LeConte, father of Joseph Nisbet LeConte, had died in Yosemite Valley a week earlier. The trip went on, of course, and Colby deemed it so spectacularly successful that he immediately drew up plans for a second excursion the following summer.

During the succeeding years, Club members, limited to about 200 per trip, repeatedly visited the most accessible areas of the Sierra: Yosemite, Kings Canyon, and the Mount Whitney region. On a trip to the latter in 1903, 103 outing members reached the highest point in the United States on the same day, a feat that William Fredric Badè, the chronicler of that year's outing, thought was "one of the most remarkable achievements in the history of mountaineering." Clarence King surely would have agreed.

The 1907 outing was a typical one. As usual, there had been a tremendous amount of behind-the-scenes planning during the preceding months. The exact itinerary had to be charted; packers and cooks had to be hired well in advance; and, at the last minute, the foodstuffs had to be purchased and packed. Will Colby handled most of this work himself, as he had done since 1901 and would do until 1930.

The locale chosen for the main base camp of 1907 was that marvelous blend of forest, rock, meadow, and water: Soda Springs, in Tuolumne Meadows. This was not unknown territory; Club members had been charmed by its pristine beauty in 1901 and again in 1904. The group spent a week at the idyllic site, then began working south across the Cathedral Range toward the headwaters country of the Merced River, territory previously unvisited by the Sierra Club. Strings of pack animals transported the paraphernalia necessary for the self-contained expedition. Huge iron stoves, cooking pots, bedding, and vast amounts of foodstuffs—all had to be balanced carefully onto the mules' backs. Packers, cooks, and their assistants broke camp as soon as possible after breakfast and traveled at a steady, rapid rate in order to have the next camp established by the time the outing participants arrived singly or in small groups.

Following dinner each night, the group would gather around a gigantic campfire to enjoy a program that might include lectures by eminent men of science, yarns spun by Civil War veterans, and performances by talented musicians. Group singing and hot drinks capped the evening's entertainment. Then, if one were fortunate, the almost unnaturally brilliant glow from the rising full moon would light the way to a soft bed beneath the lodgepole pines, the swift stream nearby providing that sublime neutral murmur that not only dampens the footfalls of unseen nocturnal creatures but also lulls one to sleep even before the myriad events of the day can be absorbed.

While most of the 1907 outing members fished and enjoyed short hikes in proximity to the camp at Washburn Lake, fifteen intrepid climbers loaded five-days' worth of food onto their backs and headed east over virtually uncharted country toward distant Mount Ritter. Their pioneering route, now a segment of the High Route, crossed Blue Lake Pass, descended remote Bench Canyon to the North Fork of the San Joaquin River, and surmounted the steep but lovely shelves and slabs rising toward Mount Ritter. The previous winter's snowfall had been the heaviest since the harsh winter of 1894–95, and the trekkers found much of their route buried by snow. Nevertheless, in short order, all fifteen climbers stood atop the famous peak first climbed by their club's president thirty-five years earlier. Some days later, after all the outing members were reunited, Colby led them down the wild gorge of the Tuolumne River to civilization. The month-long outing of 1907 was over.

One of the participants in the knapsack trip to Mount Ritter was Marion Randall Parsons, a strong-willed woman who later wrote numerous eloquent articles for the *Sierra Club Bulletin.* Parsons especially craved Mount Ritter's summit on this trip, for she well remembered an event that had taken place three years earlier, when her "feminine aspirations toward that very mountain were crushed by the stern masculine decree that fair ladies' backs were not fitted to bear such burdens. . . ." Needless to say, Parsons had no trouble with the routine ascent; indeed, she reveled in the "mysterious atmosphere" of the heights.

Women were welcomed on the Sierra Club outings, even if they often were discouraged from participating in strenuous activities. Females had been infrequent visitors to the timberline country in the nineteenth century, for there was widespread speculation that they couldn't withstand the rigorous life. Theodore Solomons had visited Tuolumne Meadows with four college women in 1896, finding them "considerably slower than athletic young men, but fully as able otherwise to cope with all the physical difficulties. . . ." For its day, this was a remarkably liberated belief, and not all of the male authors who later wrote for the *Bulletin* subscribed to this view of women's qualifications. Mount Humphreys, according to one writer, was "too dangerous to be undertaken by the ladies." Another climber wrote that before embarking on a side trip to a rugged area, "it was heartily agreed (by the boys) that the girls should be left behind to rest."

Women who wrote for the *Bulletin* generally accepted their second-class roles with good humor. Elizabeth Cowles once wrote a five-page treatise entitled, "Have You a Mountain Widow in Your Home?" This article, directed toward male mountaineers, counsels them to introduce women to the timberline country slowly, with the eventual goal of sharing the mountain experience. Even though the gist of Cowles' article is admirable for its time, hikers of the 1980s may be amused by some of the advice:

"Praise her endlessly." "Tell her how purty she looks." "Read aloud." And, if it rains for a solid week, "take your girl friend back to the valley where she can get a hot bath and go to the movies. . . ."

Women were not the only ones subjected to discrimination during the early years of Sierra exploration. Even the sainted Will Colby was not free from prejudice, as evidenced by some of his recollections published in the 1931 *Bulletin.* Charlie Tuck was a Chinese who served as an extremely able and popular cook for the first thirteen outings. "Poor Charlie" found himself lost on several occasions, episodes that Colby attributed to the demon rum: "I can testify that Chinese gin must be a very potent intoxicant." When Tuck died, "he left, for all his Mongolian ancestry, many devoted admirers. . . ." For the 1920 outing the Sierra Club had hired as chief cook a Southern black named Colonel Jones: "He brought with him as his help three other darkies, who were as incompetent and lazy as he was capable and industrious." Capable, that is, except for his biscuits, which "might have served better in the bombardment of enemy trenches." In all his voluminous writings, Colby never once castigated his fellow Caucasians in this sarcastic manner; that wouldn't have been gentlemanly.

Participants in these early outings discovered that the weeks passed pleasantly and far too quickly. Forgotten were concerns about work, personal problems, and the unpleasant events already marring the new century, such as a presidential assassination, brushfire wars in the Philippines and Nicaragua, and the dreadful 1906 earthquake and fire in San Francisco (only eighty Club members managed to find time for that summer's trip). The High Sierra became more clearly understood as a result of these early outings, though much of the exploration was concentrated around the Sierra Club's favorite locales—Yosemite and Kings Canyon.

The End of an Era

The central part of the Sierra became better known to the public after the United States Geological Survey's George Davis spent the summer of 1907 charting the rugged country south of the Goddard Divide. He became the first person to cross Muir Pass with pack animals, a feat Joseph LeConte—perhaps somewhat enviously—attributed to the unusually heavy snowpack, which he thought would afford far better footing for mules than the rough talus he had looked down upon in 1904. Davis had gone on to descend the Middle Fork of the Kings River, later crossing Cartridge Pass and exploring the Mount Pinchot region. Davis's work of this summer emerged five years later with the publication of the "Mt. Goddard Quadrangle," a map regarded by many as a masterpiece of mountain cartography.

In the summer of 1908 LeConte, Hutchinson, and a Berkeley realtor named Duncan McDuffie set forth from Tuolumne Meadows with three mules and food for a month. Many segments of the high mountain route first envisioned by Theodore Solomons had been explored already, but the three men were well aware that no one yet had connected all of them. This was the trio's chief objective, but, as usual, other goals beckoned as well. For instance, halfway down the range rose the soaring crests of the Mount Abbot group; of its seven peaks, all rising above 13,000 feet, none ever had been attempted. Farther south, another feature intrigued LeConte; six years earlier, from Split Mountain, he had spied a broad gap at the head of the South Fork of the Kings River. If pack animals could be led across this barrier—now known as Mather Pass— it would shorten the route by keeping it close to the main crest; the alternate route over Cartridge Pass lay several miles to the west.

For the first sixty miles of their journey, the three men followed the familiar ground along the Middle and South forks of the San Joaquin River. Then, at Mono Creek, they turned east and headed upstream toward the northern outriders of the Mount Abbot group. From the summit of impressive Mount Mills, which they ascended from the head of the Fourth Recess, the men were stymied by the knife-edged ridge leading across to Mount Abbot, the area's prize summit. Unwilling to abandon their goal without examining the other aspects of the peak, the trio spent several days circling the Mono Divide on the west, returning to the subalpine region by means of the Hilgard Branch of Bear Creek. Their mountain proved more accessible from Lake Italy, and late in the afternoon of July 13 the men stood atop its 13,715-foot summit. There was no sign of previous ascent; indeed, LeConte felt "certain that no mountaineer had ever before been nearer than the peak of Seven Gables, six miles to the southwest." (Unaccountably, LeConte seems to have forgotten not only his own recent ascent of nearby Mount Mills, but the ascent, by both Brewer and Solomons, of Peak 12,691, two miles to the northwest.)

Returning from Mount Abbot's summit, LeConte and Hutchinson detoured to a broad saddle west of the peak. LeConte, realizing that the Second Recess probably could be reached from this pass, thought it would "make a great cut-off in the High Mountain Route." The planners of the John Muir Trail apparently regarded this gap—known today as Gabbot Pass—as impractical, with the result that it is now a wild and integral part of the High Route.

The three men continued their journey south and on July 18 successfully crossed Muir Pass, where the terrain proved even rougher than LeConte had anticipated. The three mules, the sturdiest money could buy, suffered badly, and by the end of the day their legs were caked with blood. But the terrain below became easier and easier, and in a few hours the expedition entered a great canyon that apparently overwhelmed LeConte. His article in the *Sierra Club Bulletin* is laced with praise; by turns, the canyon of the Middle Fork was "imposing," "glorious," and "beautiful." It seems altogether proper that this wild and serene place should bear the name of the person who described it so enthusiastically.

Leaving LeConte Canyon a few miles downstream, the

party turned up Palisade Creek. A reconnaissance to Mather Pass was successful, but the men realized that their mules—sure-footed though they had proved on Muir Pass—never could surmount a series of steep cliffs and gullies just below the Palisade Lakes. Disappointed by this, the group instead worked up Cataract Creek toward Cartridge Pass. The remainder of the trip followed familiar and relatively easy terrain. After crossing Pinchot and Glen passes, the trio descended to Vidette Meadow and followed Bubbs Creek to Kings Canyon. LeConte estimated they had traveled about 230 miles on the twenty-seven-day journey.

This expedition of 1908 can be said to mark the completion of significant High Sierra exploration. The route followed by the three adventurers admirably fulfilled two of the three requirements set forth years earlier by Theodore Solomons. The "high mountain route" indeed paralleled the main crest, and it had been shown that if one used care, pack animals could be cajoled along it. But in numerous places it most definitely did not meet the third requirement: it could not be called a trail.

Realizing that few persons would attempt the arduous journey until a proper trail was established—and perhaps thinking of the vast new territory that could become accessible to their annual outings—the directors of the Sierra Club suggested to the California State Legislature that it would be in the public interest to construct and maintain a trail running the length of the Sierra. In 1915 the legislature appropriated $10,000, and work soon began on the trail, named in honor of the late president of the Sierra Club, John Muir. Within a few years crews of young men had constructed a well-engineered path stretching between Yosemite and the southern ramparts of the range. Appropriations ran out before the trail could be built over two major obstacles—Mather and Forester passes. But alternate routes sufficed, and Solomons' vision of a high mountain route was, by the mid-1920s, exemplified by the 210-mile-long John Muir Trail. Francis Farquhar spoke for many outdoors enthusiasts when he wrote that the new path was "a magnificent memorial, a highway for devout pilgrims blessing the memory of the prophet who was the first to sing the praises of this glorious sequence of mountain, meadow, pass, and lake."

Another symbol of the passing of the pioneering era concerns the formal diminishing of the range's *terra incognita.* In 1912 the United States Geological Survey published the last chart of its long-awaited set of High Sierra maps. With a scale of two miles to the inch, these well-executed quadrangles enabled prospective travelers to wander through the mountains with confidence. Understandably, these new maps contained a few errors: names sometimes were affixed to mountains other than the ones intended, and streams occasionally drifted into the wrong watersheds. But the blank sections that had characterized all previous maps finally had been filled in; no longer would hikers be obligated to climb a ridge to know what lay on the opposite side.

The appearance of these new maps, combined with the

increasing ease by which the Sierra could be reached from the big cities, meant that vacationers soon thronged into the mountains, leading their pack animals along the newly charted paths. In spite of this influx, many remote sections of the timberline country remained infrequently visited during the next twenty years, for, as is true nowadays, hikers tended to congregate around beautiful locales easy of access.

Nevertheless, by the end of the 1930s, nearly every remote cirque and peak of the High Sierra had been visited, for during the period between the two world wars the last bastions of the unknown—the summits themselves —were conquered. Numerous mountain climbers of this period sought out the fine, untouched summits that had been ignored by the turn-of-the-century pioneers, but no one individual left his footprints upon so many of them as Norman Clyde. This scholar of the classics, who gave up a teaching career to spend more time in the mountains, began his Sierra climbing career in 1914, when he was in his late twenties. A half-century later he was the veteran of perhaps 1,000 ascents, of which 125 were either first ascents or new routes up previously ascended mountains.

During the 1920s and 1930s, the period of his most prolific climbing, Clyde served as a guide on numerous annual outings of the Sierra Club, thus becoming a well-known figure to many high-country travelers. An unhurried eccentric who transported a ninety-pound pack from one campsite to another, Clyde was also the detective who unerringly led searchers to the corpses of those who had come to grief on the crags. The man who sat, motionless, for hours against a lodgepole pine while absorbing *The Odyssey* in the original was also the consummate mountaineer who, without benefit of companionship, nonchalantly negotiated the vertical terrain of those very spires from which the overconfident had plummeted.

Compelling though the adventures of Norman Clyde are, one also must credit others who followed. In the 1930s a small cadre of Sierra Club rockclimbers used ropes and pitons to reach dozens of minor, but spectacular, summits scattered throughout the range. Years later, a generation of technical rockclimbers who had learned their craft on the huge walls of nearby Yosemite Valley arrived in the high country, establishing numerous multiday routes. The High Sierra—even its vertical planes of granite—was no longer a place of mystery.

Yet, from a High Route campsite at nightfall on a summer's day, the traveler of today gazes across a landscape little changed from that seen by the likes of Brewer, King, Solomons, and LeConte. As the remaining wisps of cumulus clouds dissolve in the alpenglow, the traveler might contemplate the following: the whisper of the brook in the distance soothed the pioneers also; the enormity of the full moon peering over the serrate crest astonished them also; the sudden cessation of the afternoon's breeze calmed them also. And, during this reverie, the traveler might—for a few moments—be transported gently back in time to stand side by side with the pioneers, wondering with them what new wonders tomorrow will bring.

2

Cirque Country:

Gnarled pines on Windy Ridge; LeConte Canyon and the Sierra crest form the backdrop.

Kings Canyon to Dusy Basin

ABOUT FIVE O'CLOCK I camped for the night upon a
charming knoll of shining granite, glacier-polished,—
just across the stream from which grew plenty of feed
[for Jack, the mule]. The timber line was near, and
sweeping snow-fields patched the rocky walls of the
mountains about and even below my little
encampment. From some scrubby mountain pines near
by I got bristly boughs—which Jack dragged to where
I wanted them—and I built a good bed, resting, like an
eagle's nest, upon the bare polished granite. Next came
the cheery fire; and then, after a bath in the icy stream,
I was prepared to enjoy the situation to the full,
basking in the sun and studying the view down the
cañon; for, softened as it was into a sort of mountain
dreamland—a vision of the Delectable Mountains—in
the warm haze of the afternoon sunshine, it was as
grand and as beautiful a scene as ever my eyes beheld.

Bolton Coit Brown, describing the
landscape just below Lake Basin.
From the May 1896
issue of the *Sierra Club Bulletin.*

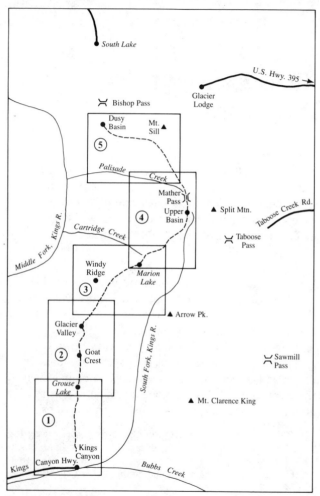

Broken line indicates approximate course of the High Route;
numbers refer to topo map sections found at end of book.

KINGS CANYON is a marvelous place to begin an adventure into the timberline country of the High Sierra. This deep gorge, dominated by enormous ramparts of granite, long has been regarded as one of the premier sights of the range. Indians traveled through the canyon on their frequent trading journeys between the great central valley and Owens Valley, and there can be little doubt that they paused often in the sublime canyon to hunt game. Even today bear and deer roam the lush floor of the valley, and trout flash up and down the South Fork of the Kings River. Travelers who walk even a short distance from the highway will find themselves in a place little altered from the sanctuary the Indians once revered.

It is somewhat of a miracle that present-day visitors are able to enjoy the canyon in such a relatively pristine state, for after a road was built to Cedar Grove, around 1910, the canyon attracted numerous sightseers, some of whom harbored inappropriate thoughts. "Attempts have been made by certain irrigationists," wrote William Colby in 1926, "to secure permits to flood the Kings River Cañon. . . . It should be borne in mind that if these water-permits are once granted this region will be irrevocably mutilated and its value for national recreational purposes materially diminished for all time." The Sierra Club—ably represented by such farseeing men as Colby, Ansel Adams, Francis Farquhar, and Joel Hildebrand—campaigned for many years to save the canyon from exploitation, and finally, in 1940, Congress established Kings Canyon National Park. Yet even as late as 1952, the city of Los Angeles, that voracious user of water, had on file an application to construct a 155-foot-high dam on the Kings River just west of Cedar Grove, the village at the park boundary. This dam, and two additional dams planned for upstream, not only would have drowned Kings Canyon, but would have created a series of reservoirs extending into the very heart of the High Sierra. The project needed the upstream dam sites to be workable; fortunately, these were located inside the park, and the water-power brokers turned their attention to other rivers.

Thus, instead of watching water-skiers at play upon a placid reservoir, the High Route traveler leaving road's end is able to appreciate a more pleasant vista: the glistening Kings winding silently through Zumwalt Meadows. The initial objective is to surmount the Monarch Divide, the watershed boundary between the South and Middle forks of the Kings River. Once this lofty ridge is attained, the High Route closely parallels it eastward as it becomes known as Cirque Crest.

The word "cirque" in this place name proves accurate, for the traveler constantly walks up or across these common Sierra features. The French word—derived from the Latin *circus,* or ring—cannot be rendered accurately into English. Perhaps "basin" and "amphitheater" come closest, but a basin can contain numerous cirques and an amphitheater is generally smaller and steeper-sided than a cirque. In essence, a cirque is a huge scoop in the flank of a mountain ridge. Ridges, or spurs, enclose the cirque on two sides; only the downhill side is open. This gap, of course, marks the exit path of the glacier responsible for carving the feature. The observant hiker can spot telltale traces of the former glacier in the form of highly polished granite slabs. More often than not, a lake or two reposes in the bottom of a cirque, adding to the charm of these geological wonders.

Cirque Crest and its extensions continue east to meet the main Sierra crest near Mather Pass. The High Route weaves through cirques and basins, crosses rugged ridges, and finally meets the John Muir Trail just south of the pass. After following this famous path north for half a dozen miles, the High Route once again strikes out cross-country, traversing three passes before reaching Dusy Basin, the northern terminus of this segment of the route.

During the entire journey the hiker travels in the watershed of the Kings River. This turbulent stream, with its three major forks, dominates the geography of the south-central Sierra. The High Route trekker will not encounter the North Fork, for it lies far to the west of the main crest. He or she will, however, step across the other two rivers at their respective sources, a privilege reserved only for those who have walked many miles through a fabulous mountain wilderness.

Approaches

Kings Canyon, the southern terminus of the High Route, can be reached easily by following California State Highway 180 eastward from Fresno. The canyon's main administrative area, Cedar Grove, is reached about seven miles before the highway ends. Permits and advice can be obtained at the Cedar Grove ranger station; a small store and several campgrounds are located nearby. The initial few miles of the High Route follow the Copper Creek Trail, which begins from the upper parking lot at road's end.

Hikers wishing to join the High Route from U.S. Highway 395, east of the Sierra crest, should use the Taboose Pass Trail; the approach road for this rugged path leaves the highway between the towns of Big Pine and Independence. After ten miles the trail ends at the John Muir Trail; head north on this and join the High Route in Upper Basin.

Dusy Basin, the northern terminus of this segment of the High Route, can be reached in short order via the Bishop Pass Trail. See the "Approaches" section of Chapter 3 for details of this approach.

Loop trips can alleviate transportation problems considerably. Two of the most obvious trips can be made as follows. Hike the High Route until it intersects the John Muir Trail in Upper Basin, then head south on this famed path until reaching either the Woods Creek Trail or the Bubbs Creek Trail—both lead down into Kings Canyon. The second loop follows the High Route all the way to Dusy Basin, then drops into LeConte Canyon. Follow the Middle Fork of the Kings River thirteen miles downstream to Simpson Meadow, where a trail surmounts the Monarch Divide and drops into Kings Canyon.

The High Route

Kings Canyon to Grouse Lake

It is hardly surprising that the initial stage of most mountain journeys involves laborious uphill hiking. Coming at a time when the typical hiker is out of shape, unacclimated, and transporting the heaviest load of the entire trip, the seemingly endless hillsides can elicit grumblings from even the hardiest backpackers. The first section of the High Route qualifies as a splendid example of such unremitting travel, for the hiker must toil up 6,000 feet to the first major pass, a disheartening prospect enjoyable only to masochists.

Optimistic hikers who seek out the brighter side of unpleasant situations, however, will quickly discover mitigating factors on this interminable slope. The well-manicured trail zigzags up the north wall of Kings Canyon with such a gentle gradient that the traveler can slip into a rhythmic pace where the miles pass far more quickly than would be possible on a steeper, rockier path. Thus freed from scrutinizing the terrain immediately ahead, the hiker can better appreciate the two striking formations on the opposite side of the canyon. Directly across the way towers the enormous façade of Grand Sentinel, rising 3,500 feet above the meadows lining the valley floor. A few miles to the east lies the sculpted oddity known as the Sphinx, a delicate pinnacle capping a sweeping apron of granite. These two landmarks, visible for much of the ascent to the Monarch Divide, offer travelers a convenient means of gauging their progress; for instance, when one is finally level with the top of the Sphinx, the upward journey is two-thirds complete.

Hikers able to identify common Sierra trees have yet another method of measuring their progress, for the Copper Creek Trail, beginning at 5,000 feet from the end of the Kings Canyon Highway, ascends through numerous life zones, each of which is distinguished by a dominant conifer. On no other section of the High Route is the backpacker able to observe, during the space of a single day, such a variety of cone-bearing trees. One of these, the pinyon pine, will not be seen again during the remainder of the High Route, for it is absent from the western slope of the range north of this region. The observant hiker can spot several pinyon pines alongside the trail not far above road's end. Much more prominent during the early stages of the trek are the noble ponderosa pines, which rise amidst vast thickets of manzanita and black oaks. These enormous evergreens, common on the western slope below 7,000 feet, are also unusual along the route, for they are replaced at higher elevations by the similar Jeffrey pine. Two other conifers—sugar pines and white firs—also are rarely seen along the High Route; they, too, prefer lower elevations. Specimens of these two trees can be found along the first few miles of the trail.

At 7,800 feet the path crosses a year-round stream at a place indicated on the topo map as Lower Tent Meadow. Hikers anticipating a brief respite from their tedious uphill journey will be sorely disappointed upon arrival here, for they will discover not a trace of a flat, grassy patch. As if to compound the euphemism, Upper Tent Meadow, a mile farther along, is even less of a meadow; it contains numerous willows and aspens bordering a creek that rushes down a fifteen-degree incline. Only a pilot flying overhead would call this light green swath of vegetation a meadow.

Regardless of the inappropriate nomenclature, both "meadows" offer travelers an excellent opportunity to shed their packs and examine the nearby conifers. Red firs make their first High Route appearance near the lower site; at the upper one, it is by far the dominant tree. The fir's Latin name, *Abies magnifica,* seems particularly suited for this stately giant, and the traveler well might agree with John Muir's assessment: "Even in the Sierra, where so many noble evergreens challenge admiration, we linger among these colossal firs with fresh love, and extol their beauty again and again, as if no other in the world could henceforth claim our regard."

Shortly beyond Upper Tent Meadow, a marvelous view opens up to the east. Three striking horns of granite pierce the sky eight miles distant. The sharp pyramid on the left is Mount Clarence King, one of the range's most difficult summits. The less spectacular peak to its right is Mount Cotter; farther right yet lies Mount Gardiner, displaying a tremendous western escarpment. All three of these jutting formations were named in honor of members of the California Geological Survey, which in 1864 explored the Kings Canyon region. Farther south, across the great canyon of the South Fork, are the massive peaks that make up the northern section of the Great Western Divide, the most significant subrange in the Sierra. It was from one of these peaks, Mount Brewer, that two members of the Survey spotted a lofty summit that they knew instantly must be the highest point in the state. They christened it Mount Whitney, in honor of the titular leader of the Survey.

Above the 9,500-foot mark the enormous red firs give way gradually to two new High Route evergreens, the western white pine and the lodgepole pine. The trunk of this latter conifer is smooth and ramrod-straight in this vicinity, as befits its common name; only at higher elevations, where it is more exposed to the wind, does the tree live up to its Latin name, *Pinus contorta*. The tree can be recognized by its distinctive needles, which grow in pairs and are extremely sharp.

At the 10,250-foot level, amid an extensive stand of lodgepole pines, the trail finally levels off in a broad saddle offering a view westward toward Comb Spur. This welcome resting spot marks the beginning of a truly adventurous portion of the High Route, for here the hiker leaves the trail to begin wandering cross-country through the subalpine landscape. For the next thirty-five miles— mostly trailless—the High Route traveler almost always remains above the 10,000-foot level.

Leave the Copper Creek Trail at the saddle, contour north through the open lodgepole forest for half a mile until reaching the long meadow that borders the creek dropping from Grouse Lake, then ascend gentle terrain to the lakeshore. This pleasant body of water occupies the floor of a lovely cirque, the first of many such glacial basins to be encountered by the High Route traveler. Hikers wishing to add yet another conifer to their ever-growing list can easily spot the whitebark pine, the five-needled conifer that shares the shoreline with the lodgepole. These two evergreens are by far the most common trees along the High Route; not a single day passes without one or the other's presence.

Grouse Lake to Goat Crest Saddle

Work around either shore of Grouse Lake, then begin ascending north toward Grouse Lake Pass, the obvious low saddle northeast of Peak 11,354. Shortly after leaving the lake, the traveler encounters typical High Route terrain for the first time. Grassy benches and ramps, surrounded on all sides by shimmering granite, offer remarkably easy upward progress. Wildflowers and dwarf willows cover the landscape. Ancient snags, carved and etched by howling winter winds, pierce the unbelievably blue sky. Coming so soon after the monotonous, forested trail, this classic example of timberline country seems especially wondrous.

From the 11,050-foot Grouse Lake Pass there is a superb view. To the south, beyond the Mount Brewer group, rise the distinct shapes of the Kaweah Peaks Ridge, that isolated group of summits that so dominate the southern Sierra. Close at hand to the east is the uninspiring mass of Goat Mountain, the highest summit of the region. Less than two miles to the west reposes marvelous Granite Lake, a pleasantly shaped body of water encircled by acres of gleaming granite slabs.

The next High Route pass is visible also, a mere mile and a half to the north. Just to the right of a cluster of three small, rocky peaks lies the U-shaped saddle known as Goat Crest Saddle. Contour northeast from Grouse Lake Pass for a few hundred feet, then angle down a gentle, grassy ramp toward the meadow-covered valley below. At about 10,900 feet, amidst a profusion of shooting stars and other flowers, cross a meandering brook. Continue north over rolling meadowlands, past Lake 10,-979, to Goat Crest Saddle, which lies midway between Peaks 11,797 and 12,059. This amazingly gentle pass, near the three-way junction of the Monarch Divide, Goat Crest, and Cirque Crest, marks the watershed boundary separating two great Sierra rivers, the South and Middle forks of the Kings River. For nearly all of its next forty-odd miles—until Muir Pass—the High Route remains in this latter watershed. As if to inform the hiker of this fact, the pass offers a magnificent view of the symbols of the Middle Fork region, the Palisade group. Etched against the skyline, exactly fifteen miles distant, this cluster of jagged peaks includes four summits over 14,000 feet.

Goat Crest Saddle to Horseshoe Lakes

The north side of Goat Crest Saddle is by no means as gentle as the southern approach, and for the first time on the High Route the hiker encounters steep and rough terrain, along with year-round snowfields. Massive aprons of granite drop abruptly toward the higher of the two Glacier Lakes, and the traveler should keep to the left on the uppermost section to avoid the even steeper slabs directly below the pass. Only the top 150-foot section is at all tricky; a short scouting trip will reveal class 2–3 slabs separating the snowpatches. Once this section is overcome, the hiker can move with alacrity down the grassy ramps leading to the lakeshore.

Turn the lake on either side via easy walking along meadows and sandy beaches. From the lake's outlet there is a completely new view of the peaks to the north. The distinctive horn on the left side of this vista is remote Charybdis, the sinister spike guarding the entrance to one of the wildest canyons in the range, the Enchanted Gorge. To its right, a few miles closer, lies the most prominent visible peak, the black and forbidding mass of the high point of the Devil's Crags. Also visible is that section of the Sierra crest running from flattened Mount Powell southeast to triangular Mount Agassiz.

Drop down glacier-polished slabs to the lower Glacier Lake, a pleasant pond surrounded by thirty-foot-high lodgepole pines. Not far below this lake, the hiker suddenly arrives at the brink of a 400-foot dropoff. The most interesting route down this steep headwall lies along the ramps at the far left, high above a raging stream. An alternate route can be followed along streamside, but this involves thrashing through willows and scrambling over huge blocks of talus. Still another alternate route proceeds down the eastern side of the creek.

Whichever route is chosen, the hiker soon arrives at the extensive meadows forming the floor of Glacier Valley. Easy strolling through a dense forest of lodgepole pines leads, after one mile, to the State Lakes Trail, a distinct path intersected at 9,900 feet. Turn right onto this trail and follow it as it ascends a steep hillside to the lowest

State Lake. The trail veers left midway along the northern shore of this lake and climbs north through the forest to the outlet of the next lake.

From this point, at 10,450 feet, the path becomes much fainter and thus harder to follow. It contours three-quarters of a mile northwest, then surmounts a short but steep hillside—an ancient moraine. At its top, a sandy flat, one should see the inobvious sign indicating the trail to Horseshoe Lakes. Follow this trail north through the open forest.

Horseshoe Lakes to White Pass

The maintained trail fades into oblivion upon reaching the first Horseshoe Lake, and the High Route traveler next embarks on a significant trailless section across an untrammeled timberline landscape replete with history. For it was from this spot, in the summer of 1935, that members of the Sierra Club's annual outing set forth upon a journey that never has—and almost certainly never will be—repeated in the same manner. More than a hundred hikers, accompanied by numerous pack animals, somehow managed to weave their way across the ridges and basins lying between Horseshoe Lakes and Lake Basin. Although this route had been scouted previously by outing managers, the three-day crossing involved laborious trailbuilding to ensure safe passage for the stock. No traces of this manmade path exist today, though an occasional rusted horseshoe still may be seen. Present-day hikers able to envision a seemingly endless chain of humans and animals traversing this hostile terrain hardly can fail to appreciate the tenacity of these robust pioneers.

Work north from the first Horseshoe Lake for a few hundred feet until meeting the largest Horseshoe Lake. Proceed north along its western shore, then begin ascending the gentle, forested slope rising to the north. Although the hiker can follow a ducked path in this area, it is not necessary, for the traveling here is remarkably straightforward. Continue north for about three-quarters of a mile until reaching an inconspicuous ridgecrest offering a view toward the Devil's Crags. Hike eastward up this ridge, keeping near the edge of the cliff that drops precipitously into Windy Canyon. The panorama increases with each step; soon, for the first time, the traveler is able to gaze straight down the great gash of the Middle Fork toward the naked hump of Tehipite Dome, one of the range's preeminent landmarks.

Continue upward along a faint path that closely follows the curving rim overlooking Windy Canyon. Shortly after passing a tarn at 11,000 feet, the path subtly crosses Windy Ridge and commences an abrupt descent down a sandy incline to the lake shown on the topo map just east of the letter "n" in "Windy."

From this beautiful pond, located at 10,800 feet, follow a wooded ledge eastward to Gray Pass, an inconspicuous saddle overlooking the valley of the South Fork of Cartridge Creek. Drop down a long, grassy gully that debouches into this infrequently visited valley, meeting the creek at approximately 10,300 feet.

Proceed upstream from a group of lakes, passing myriad granite boulders dappled with striking gray patches, inclusions known to geologists as xenoliths. Continue up the wild cirque to a circular lake at 10,500 feet, then head left up lush meadowlands and gentle ramps to the three subalpine ponds lying one mile east. In this area the hiker wanders amidst the loveliest possible terrain, where intimate streams meander through meadows dotted with granite blocks and wildflowers.

Deer are attracted to this idyllic spot also, and in late summer the traveler is almost certain to see numerous four-point bucks prowling the timberline country in search of does. On rare occasions these magnificent stags may be spotted far above timberline; perhaps they are traveling across ridges into adjoining basins.

Looking up the gentle slope to the northeast, the hiker can see the next High Route landmark, White Pass. This inconspicuous feature, lying low on the northwest ridge of Marion Peak, can be distinguished by the monolithic white slabs and blocks that comprise a relatively level saddle. Named in 1935 by the Sierra Club expedition, the 11,700-foot pass is an easy stroll from the west.

White Pass to Marion Lake

The opposite side of White Pass, however, is far more rugged. Straight across the rocky terrain to the northeast rises the obvious red cone called Red Point; to its right, at the viewer's level, lies Red Pass, the next objective. The terrain between the two passes proves far more complex than the previous section, as it involves loose blocks and circuitous class 2 slabs and gullies.

From White Pass scramble up the ridgecrest toward Marion Peak for about fifty vertical feet, then leave the ridge and begin contouring east across blocky granite. After proceeding in this manner for a few hundred yards, begin descending ramps and shallow gullies filled with debris. Continue downward until about fifty vertical feet below Red Pass; at this point the hiker can easily attain a loose but gentle slope that leads to the pass.

Upon reaching this well-named saddle (the granite has given way to rust-colored slate), the traveler can look down the opposite side and see, some 1,200 feet below, part of Marion Lake, the next High Route goal. Above and east of this sparkling body of water lies vast Lake Basin, speckled with ponds, lakes, and meadows. Beyond this basin rises the imposing ridge separating Lake Basin from Upper Basin; the High Route crosses this massive barrier at Frozen Lake Pass, the notch seen just to the right of the pyramidal peak near the ridge's left end. To the south of this notch, behind the low saddle just right of Vennacher Needle, towers the great bulk of Split Mountain, the southernmost 14,000-foot summit of the Palisade group.

From Red Pass descend an easy but tedious slope down toward Marion Lake. Snowfields linger until late season, affording excellent glissading opportunities when the snow is soft. Interspersed among the dwarf willows and grassy shelves are short sections of talus. However, there are no real obstacles in this area, and after a descent of nearly 1,000 feet the hiker reaches a meadow containing a tarn. Just below this welcome resting place is a short, steep cliff that drops precipitously into Marion Lake. Here the hiker is confronted with a choice of several gullies. Although any one of these chutes may be followed, the easiest is the one on the left. How the 1935 Sierra Club group managed to cajole their mules down this obstacle remains a mystery. One trip participant later recalled this odious gash as a "steep chimney that, at first sight, looked impassable."

On a triangular boulder near the northern shore of Marion Lake is a plaque commemorating the person for whom the lake was named, Helen Marion Gompertz Le-Conte. Although Stanford professor Bolton Coit Brown was the first to describe this beautifully situated body of water, it is Joseph N. LeConte and his wife, Helen, who are more historically associated with the feature. Using the steep and arduous sheep track up Cartridge Creek as their approach route, the pair camped at Marion Lake several times during the early years of this century. It was from this base camp that LeConte made the first ascents of three of the eleven Sierra peaks that rise above the 14,000-foot mark: Split Mountain, Mount Sill, and North Palisade. Helen LeConte, who accompanied her husband on the 1902 adventure to Split Mountain, died in 1924; the plaque was affixed the following year.

Marion Lake to Frozen Lake Pass

From the outlet of Marion Lake follow a well-worn path that winds up a hillside to meet the inconspicuous track of the former John Muir Trail. Not maintained since 1938, when the new trail was rerouted over Mather Pass, the old trail has vanished in all but a few spots, where it is surprisingly distinct.

Continue up toward Lake Basin, passing a large, L-shaped lake, to an enormous meadow at 10,800 feet. Leave the traces of the old trail here and stroll north along the western edge of the meadow until clear of the swampy section. The next major feature of the High Route, Frozen Lake Pass, is not quite visible from this point, and routefinding problems are further complicated because the next few miles are represented on three different quadrangles: Marion Peak, Mt. Pinchot, and Big Pine. Using these maps in conjunction with a careful study of the terrain, the traveler can pick out the general location of Frozen Lake Pass: it is the first deep notch to the right of Peak 12,880+, a conspicuous pyramidal peak near the northern end of the ridge that borders the basin on the east. The correct pass also is identifiable as the second one north of

Vennacher Needle, the imposing (but not needlelike) mass near the middle of the same ridge.

From the meadow proceed northeast up gentle timber-line country, aiming for the lower right edge of the pyramidal peak. When abeam this feature, at about 11,600 feet, the hiker arrives at a large lake encircled by talus. (The Mt. Pinchot quadrangle depicts the southern one-third of this lake; the Big Pine quadrangle depicts the northern two-thirds.) Here, for the first time, the traveler obtains a close view of the southern side of Frozen Lake Pass, the left-hand notch of the two notches seen above the lake's end.

Frozen Lake Pass, certainly the most difficult section of the High Route, has a fascinating history. In 1902 the two LeContes and Curtis Lindley knew they must cross the rugged barrier separating Lake Basin from Upper Basin if they were to reach their goal, Split Mountain. On July 23, Lindley, climbing solo, reached what is now Vennacher Col, the broad saddle just south of Vennacher Needle. Undoubtedly shaken after surmounting the exposed class 3 cliff leading to the col, Lindley must have given the opposite side only a cursory glance, for that night he informed the LeContes that "the eastern side of the divide was a precipice." (In reality, he had climbed the hardest section; the east side is class 2.)

On July 24 the threesome decided to explore the ridgecrest north of Vennacher Needle. Climbing a steep, loose talus slope to the right-hand notch visible from Lake

11,600, they found that the opposite side was truly a precipice, one far too dangerous to descend. Frustrated once again, the trio decided to traverse across the steep and unpleasant terrain to the next pass north. Here, to their "inexpressible joy," the pioneers looked down a steep but passable slope covered with talus and snowfields. The way to Upper Basin would not be easy, they knew, but at least no cliffs intervened. After their success on Split Mountain the following day, the LeContes and Lindley recrossed Frozen Lake Pass. But no one revisited the 12,350-foot notch until 1922, when Chester Versteeg named it after the perpetually ice-covered tarn just below the pass on the north. By 1980 only seven more parties had signed the historic register that reposes in a cairn astride the pass.

The obvious route from Lake 11,600 to Frozen Lake Pass involves steep but fairly solid talus. Hikers should take their time, carefully testing the stability of all boulders they plan to use. The party also should spread out horizontally so that any loosened blocks will crash harmlessly below.

Upon cresting the pass the traveler gazes straight across the barren, lake-dappled tundra of Upper Basin toward enormous Split Mountain, less than four miles distant. The view to the south is spectacular also, with dozens of peaks, mostly unnamed, piercing the skyline. Directly in line with Cartridge Pass, a well-known landmark on the former John Muir Trail, rises Arrow Peak, easily recognized by its knife-edged ridges.

Frozen Lake Pass to Cirque Pass

The terrain on the north side of Frozen Lake Pass is far more rugged than that encountered on the south side. The initial class 2–3 slope, quite steep, contains extremely unstable rock, and it is difficult to avoid instigating small rockslides. Hikers should move one at a time during this nasty descent, once again making sure that no one lingers in the fall line below. Fortunately, this traumatic section is short, and the traveler soon reaches a permanent snowfield that provides safe glissading in the afternoon, when the snow is soft.

Shortly after passing the frozen tarn, the hiker arrives at yet another disheartening dropoff. Diagonal left while descending this 300-foot talus slope, aiming for a round lake at 11,500 feet. This feature signifies the end of the difficult crossing; the traveler finally has reached the appealing landscape surrounding the headwaters of the South Fork of the Kings River.

Work east across the flower-covered tundra of Upper Basin, heading in the direction of Split Mountain. After one mile the hiker intersects the High Sierra's most famous manmade feature, the John Muir Trail. Hikers who follow this well-worn path to the south will stand atop Mount Whitney in sixty miles; the trail's other terminus, Yosemite Valley, lies 150 miles to the north. During their journey to Yosemite National Park, High Route trekkers will follow the John Muir Trail for a total of about thirty miles, staying within a few air miles of it for much of the remaining distance.

Follow the trail north toward Mather Pass, the distinct saddle visible a mile away. Soon after striding up the superbly constructed switchbacks on the south side of the col, the backpacker stands astride the saddle, ready to reexplore the Middle Fork region. The views from the 12,100-foot pass are striking, especially to the north, where the dark spikes of the Palisade group dominate the panorama. Nestled in the fiordlike glacial canyon in the foreground are the two Palisade Lakes, bordered on the northeast by the serrated bulk of Middle Palisade.

Mather Pass first was visited in 1897, when a sheepman apparently negotiated the rough crossing with his burro. By the early 1920s it was certain that the John Muir Trail would be rerouted over the lofty saddle, named in 1921 in honor of Stephen Mather, the first director of the National Park Service. For various reasons, it was not until 1938 that the last link of the famed trail was built, capping an effort that had begun nearly a quarter of a century earlier.

After dropping abruptly from the pass, the John Muir Trail levels out as it approaches the Palisade Lakes. When opposite the upper lake, the hiker obtains a fine view of the next High Route landmark, Cirque Pass. This saddle can be spotted high above the grassy, slab-covered cliff rising above the far end of the lower lake.

Leave the trail about 100 yards beyond the outlet of the lower lake and begin diagonaling upward to the west, aiming for the grassy cliff seen a few hundred feet above.

There are several ways to ascend this 300-foot-high barrier, most of which involve short stretches of class 2–3
scrambling. One of the easiest routes lies at the far left,
where talus-covered shelves zigzag up the left edge of the
cliff. Those who attempt the central portion of the cliff
should expect to encounter exposed class 3 sections between wet, grassy slabs.

After topping this steep obstacle, the High Route hiker
will have little trouble following the gently angled slabs
and gullies that lead, after 1,000 feet, to the obvious, broad
saddle northeast of Peak 12,220. Cirque Pass, at 12,100
feet, offers an excellent view south toward the jagged,
unnamed peaks west of Mather Pass. To the north, mighty
North Palisade dominates the horizon, its precipitous
cliffs towering above the next High Route obstacle, Potluck Pass. In the foreground lies barren Lake 11,672, an
enormous body of water that occupies most of the floor of
the classically shaped cirque west of Palisade Crest.

Cirque Pass to Knapsack Pass

From Cirque Pass drop down a few feet toward the
lake, then begin diagonaling left down a series of intercon-
nected shelves. By looking around carefully in this area,
the hiker can avoid class 3 sections. Within a few hundred
feet the terrain eases, and the traveler soon stands at the
pleasant outlet stream of Lake 11,672. It was along this
beautiful watercourse—now known as Glacier Creek—
that Joseph LeConte, James Hutchinson, and two com-

panions tramped in 1903 during their quest for the highest summits of the Palisades.

Cross the outlet, stroll across lovely, glacier-polished slabs, then ascend a narrow, grassy slot on the minor knoll rising immediately to the north. Work northeast along the top of this hill until it is feasible to drop down toward the small lake nestling beneath Potluck Pass, the low, flat saddle northeast of Peak 12,692.

From afar, the upper part of this pass looks impassable because of steep, monolithic cliffs. In reality, however, hidden-from-below ledges afford a surprisingly easy class 2 route. Ascend an inconspicuous path up a short, unpleasant scree slope lying left of the cliffs that drop from the pass. When the path fades, follow a series of narrow shelves that slant up and across to the saddle.

Due north, only one mile distant, looms the complex southwest wall of North Palisade. One can only wonder why the 1903 pioneers, upon reaching this vantage point, didn't abandon their effort, for no obvious route exists on the craggy, 1,500-foot face. Apparently undeterred by the sobering sight, the men worked their way over to the base of the wall, discovered a hidden chute, and managed eventually to stand atop the Sierra's third-highest summit.

Two miles west of Potluck Pass, across huge Palisade Basin, lies the next High Route saddle, Knapsack Pass. Five hundred feet lower than Potluck, it is the rounded saddle just left of pyramidal Columbine Peak. A circuitous but easy section of the High Route now begins: the crossing of Palisade Basin and Knapsack Pass. Virtually no talus is encountered, and the gradient proves tame in comparison with the rugged segment just completed.

From Potluck Pass contour directly toward North Palisade, aiming for an inconspicuous saddle at approximately the same altitude as Potluck and three-quarters of a mile distant. After reaching this flattened saddle begin a gradual but roundabout descent to the largest Barrett Lake, which is met at its southeast shore.

Following a rudimentary path, circle this deep blue body of water on its east and north sides. Upon reaching the northwest side of the lake, climb a small bluff and descend gentle slabs west to the next lake, a fine place to pause and absorb the panorama. In the foreground to the south lies a strikingly beautiful lake that snakes through a small canyon. Farther south, across the enormous trench of Palisade Creek, rise the great peaks surrounding Amphitheater Lake. Dominating the view to the east is the fearsome, mile-long wall stretching between Thunderbolt Peak and North Palisade.

Knapsack Pass, lying only a few hundred feet above the level of the lake, is now prominent to the west. Wander up and across slabs, talus, and gullies via any of numerous possible routes—all circuitous—to the saddle, at 11,673 feet. Looking northwest from this pleasant site, the hiker obtains a superlative view of one of the Sierra's most distinctive subranges, the Black Divide. Near the northern end of this nine-mile-long ridge rises the dark bulk of

Black Giant, a peak soon to be seen at close range by the High Route traveler. Closer at hand, in line with this prominent peak, lies the glaciated gorge of LeConte Canyon, which curves westward toward Muir Pass, a lofty saddle hidden behind Black Giant.

Knapsack Pass to Dusy Basin

A straightforward class 2 route zigzags down the granite slabs below Knapsack Pass toward the chain of lovely lakes in lower Dusy Basin. As one approaches these shallow ponds, stands of conifers offer a welcome respite from acres of granite. Without any question, Dusy Basin is the most verdant High Route locale since Marion Lake.

Because of the basin's beauty, and because the nearest road is only eight miles away, the site has attracted hordes of backpackers and fishermen over the years; many of these wilderness lovers unwittingly have left traces of their visits. Blackened boulders are evidence of once-roaring campfires; trampled dusty areas, further marred by trenches, denote former tent platforms.

Thus, for the first time since leaving the environs of Kings Canyon, the High Route traveler encounters an area that shows obvious signs of abuse. Fortunately, wilderness authorities have reacted to this damage: quotas presently limit the number of backpackers who may visit Dusy Basin. In addition, lucky permit holders are not allowed to build campfires. These regulations, coupled with backpackers' new awareness of the wilderness ethic, should mean that this beautiful region will suffer little further damage.

This segment of the High Route ends at Lake 10,734, a shallow pond surrounded by sedges, wildflowers, and granite slabs.

Reversing the Route

The first problem encountered while traveling the High Route north to south occurs in Dusy Basin, where the traveler must locate Knapsack Pass. This is not too difficult if the hiker begins from Lake 10,734, the lowest lake in the basin. Looking southeast from here, the viewer can easily spy a rounded saddle just right of the bold pyramid of Columbine Peak. The route to the pass itself involves straightforward class 2 slabs and gullies.

From Knapsack Pass do not drop down too far before beginning to diagonal left toward the next-to-largest Barrett Lake. After circling the basin's largest lake on its north and east shores, work eastward up complex terrain undistinguished by major landmarks. When directly beneath mighty North Palisade, however, the hiker is afforded a close view of Potluck Pass: it is the easy-to-reach saddle immediately left of ragged Peak 12,692.

The descent from Potluck Pass appears steep and difficult, and it can be if the easiest route is not found. From the pass, walk down a long, diagonal ramp leading southwest. When this fortuitous feature vanishes, scramble down a series of easy, interconnecting shelves leading in the same general direction. After a short distance the hiker attains a scree slope leading downward to much easier terrain.

From nearby Lake 11,672 the route to Cirque Pass is not at all obvious. From the outlet of the lake climb up and slightly right for about 100 vertical feet. At this point it is possible to follow a series of connected granite shelves that diagonal up and left to the low point northeast of Peak 12,220.

The final routefinding problem encountered before reaching the John Muir Trail occurs just above the lower Palisade Lake. There the hiker must descend a slabby, 300-foot-high cliff. The easiest route probably lies at the far right, where class 2–3 terrain leads down toward a small, white dome visible below.

Locating Frozen Lake Pass is easy if the traveler begins looking for it from the series of trailside tarns just south of Mather Pass. As seen from here, the correct pass is the second deep notch to the right of the most prominent peak to the southwest, Vennacher Needle. Exactly where the hiker leaves the trail to head for this pass is immaterial, since the tundra of Upper Basin makes for generally easy walking. The ascent to the pass itself is fairly obvious from below.

Few routefinding problems are found on the next section to Marion Lake, but here the High Route hiker faces a dilemma. Rising above the western shore of the lake are four major talus chutes. The easiest route lies in the second-from-right gully, where a faint path may be followed. The other chutes are all passable, but they are longer, steeper, or looser.

The next problem makes itself known at Red Pass, for the terrain on the west side is complex and landmarks are few. Drop down about fifty feet from the pass, then begin gently ascending across class 2 gullies and shelves. When White Pass is first seen, just left of several prominent, light-colored outcrops, contour across toward it, making sure the ridgecrest is reached above the pass, not below it. In this manner class 3–4 slabs can be avoided.

From the beautiful meadowlands below the west side of White Pass the hiker can pick out, across the gulf formed by the South Fork of Cartridge Creek, the next objective, Gray Pass. This minor feature can be recognized as the low, gray-colored saddle just left of two white peaklets.

After climbing a long gully to Gray Pass, contour west across a wooded bench to a lovely pond. Climb the steep hillside beyond, cross Windy Ridge, and then curve down southwest along the top of the cliffs overlooking Windy Canyon. Soon it is possible to leave this curving ridge and wander down south through a dense forest to the Horseshoe Lakes.

Farther south, be careful not to miss the creek that flows down Glacier Valley from the Glacier Lakes. This stream crossing lies about a mile below the second of the

States Lakes. At the head of Glacier Valley the imposing wall can be climbed easily on the far right, by means of wooded slabs.

From the upper Glacier Lake it is easy to recognize the next High Route landmark, Goat Crest Saddle: it is the deep, U-shaped pass to the southwest. The route to this col is rather obvious, even though the hiker must weave through massive slabs of granite and circumvent steep snowfields.

From this saddle, look carefully to find the next landmark, Grouse Lake Pass. Lower than the viewer's level, it lies just left of rocky Peak 11,354. Framed perfectly in the saddle is the distant pyramid of Mount Hutchings.

After reaching the long meadow just below Grouse Lake, make sure to contour, not descend, to the southwest. Failing to do so will cause the hiker to miss the Copper Creek Trail, an embarrassing situation.

Alternate Routes

Few alternate routes exist along this initial segment of the High Route, for vast gorges and rugged ridges dictate that the hiker generally negotiate the route as laid out. Still, there are a few choices available, and these are explained below.

Hikers wishing to bypass the lovely High Route country lying between Grouse Lake and Glacier Valley can do so by remaining on the Copper Creek Trail as it descends into exquisite Granite Basin. The trail continues north over Granite Pass, later curving east to join the High Route above Dougherty Meadow.

The mere thought of climbing over difficult Frozen Lake Pass into Upper Basin might discourage less experienced High Route trekkers. There are two alternatives to this traumatic pass: Vennacher Col and Cartridge Pass. Vennacher Col, located immediately south of Vennacher Needle, is neither as loose nor as strenuous as Frozen Lake Pass, but is technically more difficult; on the west side of the col is an exposed 100-foot cliff. Persons experienced in class 3 climbing will have no trouble with this obstacle. Upper Basin is reached in short order from the pass.

The second alternative, though far easier than either Frozen Lake Pass or Vennacher Col, requires a significant detour from the High Route. This variation, indicated on the topo map as a trail, follows the traces of the former John Muir Trail over Cartridge Pass, descends 2,000 feet to the South Fork of the Kings River, and continues up this stream into Upper Basin. The old trail is difficult to follow in places, and the hiker will encounter short stretches of talus.

Mountaineering en Route

Goat Mountain

One of the great Sierra viewpoints is a peak with such a prosaic name that it often is overlooked by hikers. Goat Mountain, easily accessible from Grouse Lake via class 2 terrain, probably was climbed by James Gardiner and Charles Hoffmann during the Survey of 1864; they reported reaching a lofty peak in this area. The isolated 12,207-foot mass soon attracted curious hikers. Helen Gompertz (who later married her old friend, Joseph LeConte), climbed it in 1896, remarking that "others have already called attention to the fine panoramic view of the whole Sierra uplift from this peak, and our subsequent trips to higher mountains in no wise interfered with the verdict that the Goat Mountain view is unsurpassed in its kind." Naturally, the "whole Sierra uplift" is not visible, but the entire fifty-mile section of the crest lying between the Whitney and Evolution groups stands out sharply against the eastern sky. To the south, across the 7,200-foot-deep trench of the South Fork of the Kings River, rise the lofty peaks of the Great Western Divide.

Windy Point

Another classic Sierra vantage point, reached by a mere half-hour, level detour from the High Route, is Windy Point. Indicated on the map simply as Peak 11,150, this bump at the northern end of Windy Ridge provides a stupendous view of the gorge of the Middle Fork of the Kings River, two miles distant and 5,000 feet below. Ansel Adams and Cedric Wright, two eminent photographers of the Range of Light, visited this viewpoint during the Sierra Club's outing of 1935; several of their magnificent photographs were published in the next year's annual *Sierra Club Bulletin*. To reach Windy Point, leave the

High Route as it crosses Windy Ridge and walk out the spur to the "summit," a pleasing group of weathered granite boulders. The aesthetics of this outcrop are somewhat marred by the presence of an unmanned government experimental station.

Marion Peak

Marion Peak, offering yet another sublime view, can be reached from the High Route by following the well-delineated class 3 ridge rising above White Pass. The highest point along Cirque Crest, it was climbed first in 1902 by Joseph LeConte and Curtis Lindley; the two pioneers ascended from Marion Lake to reconnoiter the surrounding countryside.

Peak 11,553

A minor summit commanding a striking view of Lake Basin and the great canyon of Cartridge Creek is Peak 11,553. This viewpoint, first reached by Bolton Coit Brown in 1895, can be climbed from Marion Lake in the following manner: walk around the east shore of the lake, ascend alongside the obvious creek nearly to the next higher lake, then wander up the class 2 slabs and talus above. The summit is reached in short order. The escarpment on the north side of the peak is most impressive.

Mount Ruskin

Mount Ruskin, the southernmost point of the jagged ridge separating Lake Basin from Upper Basin, is a stimulating class 3 scramble from Cartridge Pass. Bolton Coit Brown described his 1895 ascent as "the most aerial and dangerous climbing that I ever happened to attempt." Regarding his handholds, the professor supposed that "an inch or two of solid rock is as safe as a yard or two—but somehow you don't feel the same about it." Present-day climbers still encounter Brown's "aerial" sections, but there are no real difficulties on the long, curving ridge.

Split Mountain

The easiest major peak in proximity to the High Route proves to be 14,058-foot Split Mountain. The standard route leaves the John Muir Trail a few miles south of Mather Pass and proceeds past Lake 11,599 to the broad saddle separating Mount Prater from Split Mountain. Horses were taken to this point during a 1943 survey, which indicates the lack of difficulty thus far. Basketball-sized talus perched at a thirty-degree angle constitutes the remaining 1,500 feet to the summit. Although often rated class 1, this slope is definitely class 2. Still, hikers encounter few problems en route to the summit, where a magnificent panorama awaits. The town of Big Pine, a dozen miles to the northeast, lies more than 10,000 feet below, and the traveler is acutely conscious of standing atop one of the earth's greatest escarpments. Genny Schumacher, editor of *Deepest Valley,* a comprehensive guide to the Owens Valley, has placed the valley into cosmic perspective: "The most dramatic shape a man on the moon could see, looking our way on a good summer afternoon at four o'clock . . . would be Owens Valley." Summit climbers able to tear their eyes away from this awesome trench can spot Mount Whitney thirty-two miles to the south; its distinctive sloping summit is visible just right of closer, multisummited Mount Williamson. To their right lie the jagged crags of that noteworthy east-west barrier, the Kings-Kern Divide. In the opposite direction, all the significant Sierra peaks as far north as the Goddard Divide loom against the sky.

Middle Palisade

Adventurous High Route hikers who are proficient on class 3 terrain will find Middle Palisade to be a rewarding ascent. Leave the John Muir Trail when approaching the lower Palisade Lake and ascend 2,000 feet of class 2 slabs and talus, aiming for the third chute left of the junction of Middle Palisade and its conspicuous southeastern spur. (Count the chute in the corner as the first.) Scramble up this steep, loose gully until it becomes steeper and more difficult, approximately three-fourths of the way to the summit ridge. Exit left in this vicinity and wander up a complex system of ledges and gullies until meeting the summit ridge. Care must be taken on this upper section, for the class 3 terrain is loose and exposed.

Mount Sill

Walter Starr, Jr., regarded Mount Sill as "the peer of all Sierra peaks in the extent and quality of its views." (Although Starr misused the word "peer" in this phrase, one easily grasps his meaning.) Generations of climbers have marveled at the unbelievable array of peaks stretching the ninety miles between Mounts Ritter and Whitney. Although the class 2 ascent has become popular nowadays, Mount Sill was once a rarely visited peak. After the LeConte-Hutchinson party made the first ascent in 1903, not a single person ventured onto the summit for twenty-two years, a curious fate for a lofty peak visible from the nearby Owens Valley. The ascent of the peak can be accomplished in just a few hours from Lake 11,672, that austere body of water covering the basin between Cirque and Potluck passes. Ascend easy terrain north of the lake until it becomes possible to enter a steep-sided cirque on the left. Work up this cirque, which contains talus and steep snow, to the ridgecrest above. The summit is then a few minutes' scramble to the east.

North Palisade

At 14,242 feet, North Palisade is the highest mountain the High Route traveler sees at close range. For this reason alone, the ascent is a rewarding one. Only mountaineers absolutely at ease on loose class 3 terrain should attempt the ascent up the southwest face, the original—and easiest—route. Leave the High Route just east of the largest Barrett Lake and ascend a tedious talus slope toward the huge chute that drops from the U-Notch, the deepest notch visible to the right of the summit. Scramble up this chute until about halfway to the U-Notch. There, at a subtle widening of the chute, the climber stands atop a bare-bottomed section of the gully. Nearby, on the left, is a narrow ledge curving around the corner. Follow this sloping shelf into the next chute and ascend it until the difficulties increase significantly. Move right into the next chute and scramble up steep rock and snow to the summit ridge. The top lies only a few steps to the left. As one might expect, the panorama from this lofty peak is extensive. But most interesting, perhaps, is the immediate foreground view of the Sierra's largest body of ice, the Palisade Glacier. Complete with bergschrunds and icy couloirs, this feature adds immensely to the alpine charm of the region.

Columbine Peak

High Route hikers unwilling to tackle the loose class 3 rock of the 14,000-foot crags of the Palisades should consider ascending Columbine Peak. The jagged ridge of talus rising above Knapsack Pass proves to be a straightforward class 2 ascent. Because of its isolated position, the 12,652-foot mass offers superb views of the Black Divide, Le-Conte Canyon, and, of course, the nearby Palisades.

Mount Agassiz

Another easy peak available to High Route hikers is 13,891-foot Mount Agassiz. Although the ascent up its western flank from Bishop Pass involves nearly 2,000 feet of talus, the patient climber is rewarded with a stunning view of North Palisade's convoluted topography.

3

Whitebark Country:

Mount Goddard rises above the boulder-strewn shores of Wanda Lake.

Dusy Basin
to Lake Italy

MANY LARGE LAKES lie in the basin's trough, some
few bright with limpid water, others glittering with
snow and little icebergs; others still dull with a thick
coating of ice that the long siege of the midsummer
day's sun is incapable of dissipating.

Such is the birthplace of the San Joaquin; such the
origin of that river which turns a hundred mills;
irrigates a million acres of grain, fruit, and vine, and
which imparts fertility and beauty to the largest and
richest of California's valleys. The Sierra crest is
nowhere grander, and nowhere more generous is the
recompense that awaits the wearied traveller, than here
among the sources of the [Evolution] Fork of the San
Joaquin.

Theodore Solomons, describing
Evolution Basin. From the
January 1896 issue of *Appalachia.*

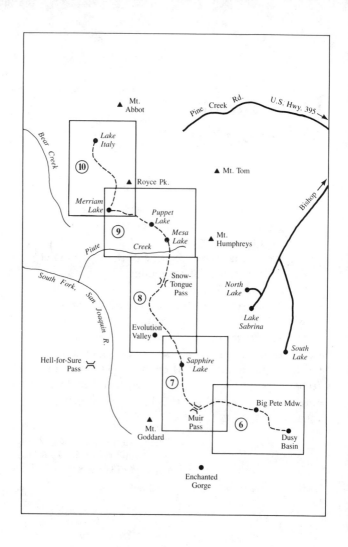

Bear Creek

Pine Creek Rd.

U.S. Hwy. 395 →

▲ Mt. Abbot

• Lake Italy

⑩

Merriam Lake •

▲ Royce Pk.

▲ Mt. Tom

Bishop

⑨

Puppet Lake •

Mesa Lake •

Piute Creek

▲ Mt. Humphreys

North Lake •

Snow-Tongue Pass

South Fork, San Joaquin R.

⑧

• Lake Sabrina

Evolution Valley •

Hell-for-Sure Pass ⋈

⑦

Sapphire Lake •

South Lake •

Big Pete Mdw. •

Muir Pass ⋈

⑥

▲ Mt. Goddard

Dusy Basin •

• Enchanted Gorge

THE TRAVELER WHO successfully negotiates the forty-odd miles comprising the second segment of the High Route passes through some of the most striking timberline country of the High Sierra. This adventure begins dramatically, for the hiker drops abruptly from the subalpine landscape of Dusy Basin into LeConte Canyon, a heavily wooded valley surrounded by towering granite formations. The traveler then follows the John Muir Trail up this curving canyon until finally topping the Goddard Divide at Muir Pass, here forsaking the Kings River watershed in favor of the vast region drained by the San Joaquin River. During the next ninety miles—all the way to the border of Yosemite National Park—the High Route weaves its way past the headwaters of the numerous tributaries and forks of this tumultuous river.

From Muir Pass the hiker follows the John Muir Trail into Evolution Basin, a glacier-scoured trench graced with some of the most attractive lakes in the range. Eschewing the trail, the High Route next crosses the Glacier Divide at rugged, historic Snow-Tongue Pass. Remaining fairly close to the Sierra crest, the route continues over hill and dale to Bear Lakes Basin, a lovely and unspoiled region containing numerous lakes named in honor of those ursine denizens of the foothills. Lake Italy, the northern terminus of this section of the High Route, lies just beyond.

The peaks and lake basins along this segment prove spectacular, but the flora along the way is fascinating also. From long distances the hiker can trace the course of streams by the pale green willows that line them. Wildflowers blanket acres of meadowlands, adding to the charm. The conifers, too, are well worth studying, especially in LeConte Canyon, where several species share trailside habitats. Higher, in the timberline country traversed by most of this segment of the High Route, one tree dominates: the whitebark pine.

Pinus albicaulis occupies a special place in the hearts of many Sierra travelers, for more than any other tree, it is the symbol of the subalpine landscape. Absent below 10,000 feet, the pine seems to seek out spectacular and lonely locations—like many backpackers. The conifer occasionally appears as an upright, normal-looking pine, but far more often has been so harassed by the elements that it resembles a shrub; indeed, its former common name was dwarf pine. John Muir regarded the whitebark as a "tree-mountaineer that climbs highest and braves the coldest blast." The naturalist discovered that even though the contorted trees are pitifully small, they can be long-lived:

one specimen, only six inches in diameter, proved to be 426 years old.

An excellent locale in which to examine the shrublike form of *albicaulis* is Mesa Lake, where it is the only pine species present. On the rocky shelves north of this remote Humphreys Basin lake, gnarled specimens appear in dense thickets. Standing in proximity to these wind-ravaged evergreens, the traveler can appreciate these words of Muir: "During stormy nights I have often camped snugly beneath the interlacing arches of this little pine. The needles, which have accumulated for centuries, make fine beds, a fact well known to other mountaineers, such as deer and wild sheep, who paw out oval hollows and lie beneath the larger trees in safe and comfortable concealment."

The whitebark pine can be recognized in two ways: by its soft-to-the-touch needles, which grow in clusters of five, and by the absence of fallen cones beneath the tree. The small cones, firmly attached to the upper branches, either disintegrate quickly on the tree when mature or are discovered by Clark's nutcrackers and chickarees—both species often are seen noisily ripping apart the cones to partake of the delectable seeds inside.

Approaches

Dusy Basin, the southern terminus of this section of the High Route, can be reached quite easily from the east via the Bishop Pass Trail, which leaves civilization at South Lake, a half-hour drive from Bishop. The eight-mile trail to the basin traverses splendid, lake-dotted country, and acclimated hikers will have no trouble reaching the High Route in one day's time.

Echo Col offers the hiker a strenuous, but direct, method of intersecting the High Route near Muir Pass. This route, beginning from Lake Sabrina on the Middle Fork of Bishop Creek, follows a well-worn trail toward Hungry Packer Lake. Just before reaching this lake, head south and ascend gentle terrain to Echo Lake, a barren body of water nestled against the Sierra crest. Snowfields and unpleasant class 2 talus then lead up to the farthest right notch of several notches on the ridge above. The final few feet to the col involve easy class 3 climbing. From the pass a tedious class 2 slope can be followed downward 1,500 feet to the John Muir Trail, which is met a mile or two below Helen Lake.

The traveler may bypass the entire southern half of this segment of the High Route by following the Piute Pass Trail west from the roadhead at North Lake. This trail, some eight miles in length, joins the High Route in Humphreys Basin, near Golden Trout Lake.

Several loop trips are available to those hikers so inclined. The longest and most varied of these trips follows the High Route all the way to Lake Italy. From here, climb over Italy Pass into Granite Park, recross the Sierra crest at the gap leading to the Royce Lakes, and descend

into French Canyon. Next, repeat the short section of the
High Route leading over Puppet Pass into Humphreys
Basin, then exit the high country via the Piute Pass Trail.
From the roadhead at North Lake, work over to the start-
ing point, South Lake, via the trail that passes George and
Tyee lakes. It also is possible, of course, to hike or hitch-
hike the dozen miles of road separating North and South
lakes.

Shorter loops—also reaching civilization at North
Lake—can be made by leaving the High Route prema-
turely and exiting the mountains at either Lamarck Col
(the class 2 pass north of Mount Darwin) or Piute Pass.

The High Route

Dusy Basin to Muir Pass

Leaving the lowest lake in Dusy Basin, the High Route
trekker joins the Bishop Pass Trail on the far side of the
Dusy Branch of the Middle Fork of the Kings River.
Within a few hundred yards this trail arrives at a viewpoint overlooking the most magnificent gorge in the High
Sierra. Named after Joseph N. LeConte, who explored
and photographed the stupendous glacial valley in 1908,
LeConte Canyon displays sculpted granite walls rising
more than 3,000 feet above its wooded floor. Most prominent of the features across the canyon are the Citadel, with
its striking north face, and Langille Peak, a cone-shaped

tower of the purest white granite. Behind these two noble peaks rises the Black Divide, its dark and gloomy peaks contrasting vividly with the shimmering granite of the lower formations.

The trail zigzags down the steep hillside falling into LeConte Canyon, twice crossing the Dusy Branch of the Middle Fork of the Kings River. Not far below the second crossing, at about 9,500 feet, the trail wanders through a sparse grove of venerable Sierra junipers. One of these, a trailside specimen with a circumference of nearly thirty feet, is without question the single most impressive tree along the High Route. Adding to the charm of this locale, the nearby stream cascades madly down an enormous granite apron toward the Middle Fork, only 800 feet below.

The path winds down the slope, reaching the John Muir Trail at 8,700 feet, the lowest point attained by the High Route since the first day of the journey. Not surprisingly at this elevation, stately conifers blanket the floor of the canyon. Turn north on the John Muir Trail, immediately passing the marked turnoff to a nearby ranger station, and meander through lodgepole pines to Little Pete Meadow, a pleasant parkland located directly underneath the towering white crags of Langille Peak.

As LeConte Canyon begins to curve west toward the Goddard Divide, the trail closely parallels the Middle Fork, by this time a mere stream. Shortly after passing Big Pete Meadow, the High Route traveler encounters, for the first time along the trek, one of the loveliest Sierra trees, the mountain hemlock. John Muir considered the graceful hemlock to be "transparently conscious of heaven and joyously receptive of its blessings." At first the hiker spots only a few of these delicate evergreens, recognized at once, even from a distance, by their droopy tips. Soon, across the Middle Fork, it is possible to pick out hundreds of well-formed specimens. By the time the backpacker reaches 9,500 feet, hemlocks share the landscape on both sides of the creek with the more familiar lodgepole pines.

Another conifer, not encountered since the first day of the trek, begins to make its appearance near this same elevation. The western white pine, a rather unusual High Route tree, can be recognized most easily by its long and relatively narrow cones, the only High Sierra cones with this distinctive shape. At about 9,700 feet the hiker passes close by the finest specimens of western white pine to be seen on the entire journey—a solitary grove of fifteen giants, each rising to nearly a hundred feet.

Not far beyond this unique group of pines, the traveler comes suddenly upon Barrier Rock, a historic landmark along the John Muir Trail. For a distance of about 100 feet the trail follows a shallow groove blasted out of an immense granite slab. This laborious task was accomplished in August 1917 by a group of restless young men who wished they were blowing up Huns rather than granite, the United States having declared war on Germany only four months earlier. "Even under normal conditions," wrote the construction boss, "it is hard to keep men at these high altitudes."

Above Barrier Rock the trail winds along upper Le-Conte Canyon through a sparse forest of mixed conifers. Dominating the view in this section, lofty Black Giant displays small, horizontal glaciers liberally sprinkled with friable black rock loosened by the elements from the sinister cliffs above. By the time the hiker reaches a small, circular lake at 10,800 feet, the only trees in sight are tiny and contorted, a sure sign that one is back in timberline country. The trail skirts the lake and begins to follow the infant Middle Fork on its final serpentine journey to its source at Helen Lake.

During the last half-mile to this huge body of water, travelers wend their way up a stream bed formed from the dark, metamorphic rock that comprises the Black Divide, here at its northernmost extension. Just beyond the outlet of Helen Lake, granite suddenly reappears: the Black Divide has been crossed.

After skirting the lake—named for one of John Muir's daughters—the hiker begins to ascend gentle but desolate country toward Muir Pass. Upon reaching this 11,955-foot saddle the traveler stands face-to-face with the classic structure known officially as the John Muir Memorial Shelter. Colloquially known as the Muir Hut, it was built during the summer of 1930, thanks to the beneficence of George Frederick Schwarz, a distinguished forestry consultant. The shelter's sturdy design was patterned after peasant buildings found in the woodless regions near the heel of Italy; the hut remains in remarkably good condition after a half-century of exposure to winter storms.

It long has been the custom for travelers to carry a few sticks of firewood from the "lowlands" to leave inside the structure in hopes that a fire may help save a life during a severe storm. Alas, nowadays there are occasional campers at the hut who burn the wood brought up by those trusting souls who remember a time when such thoughtlessness was inconceivable.

The panorama from Muir Pass is unique, for it is the only spot along the 195 miles of the High Route from which not a single tree or shrub is visible: the world consists solely of sky, rock, snow, and water. Black Giant, looking considerably less imposing than it did from the 10,000-foot level, rises to the southeast. Closer at hand is Mount Solomons, an undistinguished mass commemorating the obsessive explorer whose exploits are described earlier in this book. To the west, two dark shapes rise conspicuously: Peak 12,913 is merely a northerly extension of Mount Goddard, here hidden from view; the other black mass is ragged Mount McGee. Below this isolated mountain lies the vast expanse of Wanda Lake, named after another of John Muir's daughters.

Muir Pass to Snow-Tongue Pass

A tedious but gentle descent from Muir Pass eventually brings the hiker to the mile-long Wanda Lake. Mount

Goddard, invisible from the High Route for dozens of miles, now rises fully exposed to the southwest. The rather unprepossessing peak was a desired goal of the early Sierra explorers because of its height and isolated position. One wishes it were a more beautiful mountain.

Just below the outlet of Wanda Lake, the traveler first spies the stunningly beautiful canyon called Evolution Basin. On the right side of this canyon—and visible for the first time on the High Route since Windy Ridge—rises enormous Mount Darwin, the highest summit of the Evolution group. The 13,830-foot hulk lies at the far right end of an incredibly broken spur that juts northwest one mile from the main crest. So impressive is this 3,000-foot-high wall that its individually named summits lose their identity.

The John Muir Trail descends rocky terrain to Sapphire Lake, a cobalt blue body of water displaying an exquisite shoreline. Joseph LeConte, one of the first persons to explore this region, thought that this striking lake "lies like a jewel in its circular rock setting." The unknown poet who furthered LeConte's simile by naming it Sapphire is to be congratulated. The views from lakeside are remarkable even by High Route standards. Reddish-hued Mount Haeckel lies due east, its sharp summit cone contrasting dramatically with its more massive neighbors. The finest-looking of all the Evolution peaks, Mount Huxley, is seen here to good advantage, and the present-day traveler probably will concur with LeConte's description from his 1904 journey: "a wonderfully picturesque piece of mountain sculpture."

After descending alongside burbling Evolution Creek for about half a mile, the traveler reaches famed Evolution Lake, another jewellike feature. The trail skirts this long lake on its eastern shore, passing directly beneath the great façade of Mount Darwin. The north end of Evolution Lake long has been regarded as one of the beauty spots of the Sierra, and the conspicuous peninsula that juts into this part of the lake has everything a wilderness lover could hope for: a fabulous shoreline, several hundred twisted whitebark pines—along with a scattering of lodgepole pines—and two easy-to-climb knolls offering marvelous panoramas.

These two lumps of sculpted granite, rising perhaps 125 feet above lake level, are known to geologists as *roches moutonnées*—or, in colloquial English, "sheepback rocks." The odd features, rising boldly out of the otherwise uniform floor of the scoured valley, were spared by the glaciers that once crept through Evolution Basin. Consisting of hard, well-jointed bedrock, the domes proved compact enough to resist the glaciers, thus forcing the ice to either side. *Roches moutonnées* are uncommon in the Sierra; these two are excellent examples of this geological curiosity.

After leaving Evolution Lake the John Muir Trail descends through lovely meadowlands for about a quarter of a mile. Soon the hiker reaches the top of the dropoff overlooking the long, forested canyon called Evolution Valley. The extensive meadows dotting this well-known valley were favored campsites for members of the early Sierra Club outings because of the pleasing location and plethora of firewood.

Fifty yards or so below this viewpoint, the traveler reaches a symbolic junction, for it is at this unmarked spot that the High Route and the John Muir Trail diverge, each to head north in a radically different manner from the other. After dropping into Evolution Valley, the John Muir Trail traverses many miles of rather uninspiring countryside along the western foothills. Indeed, for its next fifty-odd miles the famous path ascends into the high country only twice, and then but briefly. During much of this monotonous, forested journey, the hiker remains half a dozen miles—or more—from the Sierra crest, totally out of sight of the spectacular peaks and lake basins of this region. By contrast, the High Route wanders cross-country through an idyllic landscape: the heart of the Sierra's timberline country.

Upon stepping off the John Muir Trail, the High Route trekker faces a long, level traverse northwest toward Lake 11,106, located north of McClure Meadow. This three-mile jaunt across a steep hillside is not really difficult, since for much of the distance the hiker simply strolls across the wooded benches fortuitously sandwiched between 10,800 feet and 11,000 feet. But the person who drops much below the lower elevation, or who climbs much above the upper height, encounters steep and sometimes impassable granite barriers. No distinctive landmarks are to be found along this traverse, so the route must be described in the most general terms. The first mile involves gentle, forested slabs and numerous easy stream crossings. The middle mile is pleasant, for the hiker contours along wooded shelves, occasionally dropping or climbing fifty feet to reach another shelf. During the last mile, the terrain starts to flatten out, but here, as the traveler begins a gradual upward traverse, he or she encounters several short but annoying swampy sections and even a few stretches of bushwhacking through wiry willows.

Eventually the hiker leaves this convoluted terrain and emerges at timberline just above—and east of—huge Lake 11,106. This lake has an interesting history, for in July 1904 James Hutchinson and three cohorts camped here en route toward their first ascent of Mount Humphreys. Naming the body of water Lake Frances, the men left their tethered pack animals behind while spending three days on their first ascent. The High Route follows exactly their pioneering route across lofty Glacier Divide.

There is no particular need to descend to Lake Frances. Instead, work northward up gentle, grassy gullies toward Snow-Tongue Pass, the conspicuous notch just right of a divide peak with two rounded summits. (On the map, this pass is located midway between Peaks 12,498 and 12,971.) Surprisingly easy walking leads past several tarns to a short, stable talus slope that ends at 12,300-foot Snow-Tongue Pass.

Here a superb view—both exhilarating and frightening

—awaits the High Route trekker. Dominating the view to the northeast, only four miles away, is the towering hulk of Mount Humphreys, by far the most imposing peak of the central High Sierra. Huge and isolated, the 13,986-foot giant proves to be one of the most difficult-to-reach summits in the entire range.

The terrifying part of the view is the immediate foreground, where acres of shattered rock drop precipitously down the northern escarpment of Glacier Divide. James Hutchinson was aghast as he gazed over this cliff in 1904, noting with gloom that "the prospects were far from bright." As with most obstacles in mountainous country, however, the sight proved worse than the actuality, and Hutchinson's group had no particular trouble with the descent.

Snow-Tongue Pass to Puppet Pass

Since the pass register indicates that some three hundred persons have crossed Snow-Tongue Pass during the last two decades, the present-day traveler should take heart and begin the descent with care, not trepidation. Do not drop straight down from the pass, for the steep main chute visible below is dangerously loose. Instead, scramble up the ridge to the south for forty or fifty feet to a small notch. Leave the ridgecrest here and carefully—one person moving at a time—drop down the slope below. After about 100 feet, the hiker is faced with a choice of routes, depending on the snow conditions. None of the possible routes are easy; all involve steep, loose rock and snow. Hutchinson's "snow tongue" lies just to the east, and if the snow is soft, the trekker can kick steps down this ever-present feature. A safer method is to cross the snow couloir and then zigzag down the steep talus and scree on the other side. Numerous variations can be followed in this area.

Fortunately, the nasty part of this class 2–3 descent lasts but 300 feet; below lies a year-round snowpatch that can be followed down to a small lake at 11,700 feet. From there, scramble down relatively stable talus to the rockbound Wahoo Lakes. From the outlet of the lower lake, the hiker is able to follow much easier terrain down to the vast flatlands comprising Humphreys Basin. Cross Piute Creek about one-half mile upstream from Golden Trout Lake and soon thereafter intersect the Piute Pass Trail.

Step across this well-trod trail and ascend gentle slopes northward. There is a paucity of landmarks during the next few miles, but by keeping Tomahawk Lake on the left and Lower Desolation Lake on the right, the hiker eventually can top a small crest and spot Mesa Lake dead ahead. This infrequently visited lake—recognized by the few dozen whitebark pines scattered above its northern shore —lies just west of the outlet of the basin's largest body of water, Desolation Lake.

From Mesa Lake ascend northeast alongside a small stream until reaching a tarn one-half mile distant. The panorama from the slopes above this tarn encompasses the entire eight-mile ridge known as Glacier Divide, and for the first time the hiker can appreciate why the John Muir Trail circumvents the ridge far to the west. Even Snow-Tongue Pass, which the High Route traveler has just crossed, looks impossible from this vantage point. Mighty Mount Darwin, poking up from behind Alpine Col, can be recognized by the sharp ribs separating the twin lobes of its glacier. Mount Humphreys, as usual, is magnificent; to its right, Mount Emerson's outline bears an uncanny resemblance to that of Mount Whitney when that peak is viewed from the northwest.

Continue ascending in a northerly direction over easy terrain to a level section of tundra that leads across to Puppet Pass, the 11,800-foot gap located just above the letter "o" in the word "FOREST" on the Mt. Tom quadrangle. A fine view opens up to the north. Directly below is boomerang-shaped Puppet Lake, occupying a wide shelf dotted with clumps of conifers. In the far distance, on the left, rises the sharp outline of Seven Gables; its dramatic right-hand skyline forms one of the most spectacular cliffs in the High Sierra. In line with this escarpment, and on the opposite side of the wide valley known as French Canyon, the traveler can spot the shimmering surface of Merriam Lake, a High Route lake only a few hours' walk from Puppet Pass. Closer at hand, and to the right of Merriam Lake, rise two huge, white talus peaks—Merriam Peak and Royce Peak. Farther right, partially blocked by a ridge, are the upper slopes of symmetrical Mount Gabb. To its right, the sharpest and most prominent summit in a cluster of peaks is Bear Creek Spire, seven miles distant. All of the peaks mentioned in this paragraph soon will be seen at close range by the High Route backpacker.

Puppet Pass to Feather Pass
The traveler who happens to be in the vicinity of Puppet Pass around noontime on an August day well might notice massive cumulus clouds roiling overhead, for nearby Mount Humphreys seems to attract a disproportionate share of the thunderstorm activity of the central Sierra. A typical thunderstorm cycle most often requires several days to complete, and a knowledgeable observer can predict the next stage simply by "reading" the sky.

Following a period of perfectly clear weather, the opening of a thunderstorm cycle is marked by the randomly scattered clouds that appear in midafternoon and dissipate by sundown. During the next few afternoons the clouds appear ever earlier and loom ever larger before vanishing impotently. The major outburst, reserved for the fourth or fifth day, allows hikers to witness an event not soon forgotten. (Don't watch this show from a summit or a ridge, or the day might turn into a shocking experience.) On this day wispy cumulus clouds, absolutely white and insignificant at first, materialize late in the morning. A few hours later the thickening masses magically coalesce, and thunderheads shoot upward with amazing rapidity to altitudes as high as 40,000 feet. The temperature drops abruptly, a brisk wind springs up, and the sun disappears behind the seething gray shapes. Thunder growls in the distance, then the heavens explode. Tendrils of lightning lick the nearby summits. An eerie darkness contrasts with the glistening hail pelting the earth. Crackling ripples of thunder foretell of impending detonations that echo forever off the cliffs. The gods seem to have lost control of their domain, and for a few minutes all is chaos.

Then, in a most subtle fashion, the lightning flashes less frequently, and the explosions fade to mere loud grumblings. Light rain begins to fall, indicating that the nucleus of the storm has moved on. Half an hour later the sun reappears, and, in the words of John Muir, "everything is refreshed and invigorated, a steam of fragrance rises, and the storm is finished. . . ."

An August day might culminate in such a storm; it also might be one of those pristine summer days when not a solitary cloud mars the horizon. In either case the hiker eventually must leave Puppet Pass and move along north.

Descend a short, steep talus slope to the meadowlands above Puppet Lake, then pass around this lake on its western shores. Continue north and drop down a gentle incline to the lake west of Moon Lake. Soon the traveler begins the long descent through a dense lodgepole forest into French Canyon. At the bottom, cross the main creek and join the Pine Creek Pass Trail. Follow this downstream until about one-half mile below the spectacular cascade that falls into the canyon from the Royce Lakes. Leave the trail near this point and begin diagonaling up a tree-covered slope, eventually reaching the extensive meadows three-quarters of a mile below Merriam Lake. After crossing this lush parkland, ascend a short incline to the lake—a pleasant, medium-sized body of water bounded on its west side by talus and on its east margin by slabs and meadows sprinkled with both whitebark and lodgepole pines.

From the north end of Merriam Lake scramble up the steep slope next to the obvious inlet cascade until reaching the sandy valley above. There, for the first time, it is possible to see Feather Pass, the next major watershed boundary on the High Route. This 12,350-foot gap proves easy to recognize, for it lies directly in line with a spectacular pinnacle that juts up from the north ridge of Peak 13,242 (Feather Peak).

Remain on the east side of the chain of lakes in the valley ahead. The terrain is remarkably gentle in this valley, and the hiker should reach the highest lake in short order. (The Mt. Abbot quadrangle mistakenly indicates the elevation of this lake as 10,925 feet; this height quite likely applies instead to Merriam Lake.) From this rock-bound lake ascend a headwall, then work up gently angled slabs to Feather Pass, the broad saddle separating Peaks 12,831 and 13,242.

Feather Pass to Lake Italy

Descend the northwest side of Feather Pass via slanting ramps and steep talus. Careful routefinding in this short section pays off; otherwise the hiker may encounter a few class 3 dropoffs. After about 150 vertical feet, the terrain levels out and sandy slopes lead down past several tarns to Bearpaw Lake. Turn this on its northern shore and, just beyond its outlet, meet the next body of water, lovely Ursa Lake. The traveler now stands in the heart of convoluted Bear Lakes Basin, a starkly beautiful region dotted with dozens of aesthetic lakes.

Stroll around the north side of Ursa Lake until the shoreline is rudely interrupted by impassable cliffs. Leave the lake here and ascend a steep, grassy gully for about 200 feet. The panorama from the top of this gully is dominated by the double-summited bulk of Seven Gables, the solitary giant first climbed by Theodore Solomons and Leigh Bierce in 1894. The foreground view reveals several of the gemlike lakes so typical of Bear Lakes Basin.

Without gaining much elevation, traverse north a few hundred yards to meet the stream emanating from Black Bear Lake. From the outlet of this austere lake—situated less than a mile from the Sierra crest—ascend complex terrain northwest past two tarns to a sandy saddle overlooking White Bear Lake. This intimate pond, ringed by vertical rust-red granite, surely ranks as one of the most soulful locales in the High Sierra.

Rising just a few feet above White Bear Lake's northwest shore is White Bear Pass, a broad saddle on the divide separating the Hilgard Branch of Bear Creek from its East Fork. When descending from White Bear Pass, aim for the willow-covered ledges down and to the right. Do not drift too far to the left unless willing to slither down class 4 slabs. Although the terrain is steep and rugged for much of the distance down to Brown Bear Lake, the hiker will find no particularly difficult or dangerous sections. During rest stops, the traveler can contemplate the enormous bulk of Mount Hilgard across the valley, or wonder how the lakes below—in a totally different watershed from Bear Lakes Basin—could possibly have been given ursine names too.

Upon reaching Brown Bear Lake, curve around its eastern shoreline via meadows and patches of talus. From the outlet of nearby Teddy Bear Lake, contour north across glacier-polished granite interspersed with isolated clumps of whitebark and lodgepole pines. The view down the Hilgard Branch of Bear Creek is magnificent, especially in the late afternoon, when the stream glistens with reflected sunlight as it drops sinuously through the willows and slabs on its journey toward the San Joaquin River. Within a few hundred feet of the High Route at this point is the campsite occupied by Joseph LeConte, James Hutchinson, and Duncan McDuffie before their first ascent of Mount Abbot in 1908.

Join the poorly maintained Italy Pass Trail just below Lake Italy and ascend a gentle incline to the lake's outlet.

Named—by the United States Geological Survey in 1907 —for its singular shape, Lake Italy is by far the largest body of water in the Mount Abbot region. It is not a particularly interesting lake; indeed, it can be argued that it is fundamentally ugly. Uninteresting peaks composed of uniform talus overlook the drab shoreline. A greater contrast between Lake Italy and the recently visited White Bear Lake hardly can be imagined. Still, the pleasure of hiking the High Route will not be unduly diminished if less-than-spectacular features occasionally mar the landscape. In any case, Lake Italy has the distinction of marking the northern end of this segment of the High Route.

Reversing the Route

The first problem to be solved by those who are traveling this segment from north to south occurs in the Lake Italy region, where the traveler must find the valley containing Brown Bear Lake. This proves easy if the hiker does not follow the trail too far below the lake. When less than half a mile below the lake, leave the trail, turn sharply left, and ascend a gentle incline to Brown Bear Lake.

Bear Lakes Basin is a convoluted region where the long-range visibility often is blocked by intervening ridges. From White Bear Pass work around the north side of White Bear Lake and ascend to the sandy saddle just east of it. From here wander down complex terrain to conspicuous Black Bear Lake. Descend its outlet stream for about 200 yards, then contour left around the hillside on easy ledges until reaching the top of a grassy gully that plunges into Ursa Lake. From this point the traveler should have little trouble finding the easiest way to Feather Pass, the deep gap to the right of the peak containing jagged pinnacles on its left-hand skyline.

There are numerous ways to travel from French Canyon to Puppet Pass. The best landmark in this region is the spectacular cascade that falls into the canyon from the Royce Lakes. Leave the Pine Creek Pass Trail when below this feature, cross the main creek, and ascend forested slopes southeast to Puppet Lake. From this austere body of water the hiker should recognize Puppet Pass as the rounded saddle lying about a mile to the southeast.

Crossing Glacier Divide from Humphreys Basin can prove traumatic if the correct pass is not located. The traveler who peruses the landscape south of the basin can spot a low saddle separating Peak 12,498—a conspicuous spur jutting north from the divide—and Peak 12,971, a rounded mass harboring several small glaciers under its north face. This saddle, Snow-Tongue Pass, proves to be one of the most difficult High Route obstacles. The route to the base of the pass is rugged but straightforward. On the final steep section keep to the left, working upward alongside a year-round snow couloir.

Once over the pass, follow gentle terrain down to the environs of Lake Frances. Here, however, further problems arise, for it is difficult to locate the best route leading onto the wooded shelves that shoot three miles across to Evolution Lake. Do not descend much more than 200 feet before beginning this long traverse to the southeast. The object is simple: stay at approximately 10,900 feet all the way across, deviating only a few score feet at a time to transfer from one bench to another.

Alternate Routes

Hikers wishing to cross the Glacier Divide at an easier pass than Snow-Tongue Pass may do so in either of two places, both relatively straightforward, well-traveled passes. These two alternates—Alpine Col and the Keyhole —both leave the High Route in the vicinity of Evolution Lake. From this lake follow the John Muir Trail for about one-half mile until reaching the first major switchback, at about 10,700 feet. There a faint path leaves the trail and immediately begins ascending the steep hillside above. Follow this path up alongside a raging creek to Darwin Bench, a lovely flat area at 11,200 feet. Continue north toward the Glacier Divide, passing two huge rockbound lakes, to the barren lake reposing immediately south of sharp Muriel Peak. Here the two routes diverge. Alpine Col, the lower of the two passes, lies on the left; from it the hiker heads to Goethe Lake, then drops into Humphreys Basin near Muriel Lake. The second pass, the Keyhole, lies to the right of Muriel Peak; this route also leads to Muriel Lake, but via the Lost Lakes. Although both passes involve ascending and descending hundreds of feet of tedious talus, no particularly traumatic sections are encountered.

Backpackers who don't mind forsaking the rigors of the subalpine landscape for a short while can discover an excellent and obvious way to do so in the Humphreys Basin region. Simply follow the Piute Pass Trail downstream to Hutchinson Meadow, a lovely, forested parkland at the junction of Piute Creek and French Canyon. From here ascend French Canyon until just beyond the creek emanating from Merriam Lake, high above. Ascend the forested slope and join the High Route in the extensive meadows below the lake.

An alternate route that bypasses Merriam Lake and Bear Lakes Basin begins in upper French Canyon. Ascend the precipitous—but easy—slope just east of the spectacular cascade that falls from the lowest Royce Lake. Follow the chain of lakes in the valley above until reaching the upper lake. The hiker then can easily cross the Sierra crest and descend into Granite Park. Here a poorly maintained trail recrosses the crest and descends to the outlet of Lake Italy, where the High Route is rejoined.

The traveler may vary the route from Bear Lakes Basin to Lake Italy in the following manner. From the sandy saddle overlooking White Bear Lake ascend northeast into a gravel-filled valley containing an elongated tarn. Continue for several hundred feet to a dropoff overlooking Jumble Lake. Steep talus leads down to this rockbound body of water, which is turned most easily on its east and north sides. Proceed down easy terrain to Lake Italy, then turn left and join the High Route at the lake's outlet. (As discussed in Chapter 4, the south shore of the lake, leading toward Gabbot Pass, is not recommended.)

Mountaineering en Route

Black Giant

Black Giant, the culminating point of the Black Divide, towers higher than all the other peaks in the vicinity and thus provides a spectacular viewpoint. Joseph LeConte, naming the mountain in 1904, commented that it "certainly commands a peerless view." But LeConte hadn't the time to attempt it, and it remained for George Davis of the United States Geological Survey to stand atop the isolated mass the following year. Reaching this lofty eminence is a simple matter: leave the John Muir Trail at the inlet of Helen Lake and scramble up the class 1 and 2 slopes comprising the northwest side of the mountain. The ascent is neither difficult nor particularly exciting, but the panorama proves worth the effort—especially dramatic is the Palisade group, some seven miles to the east.

Mount Goddard

An even finer vantage point is offered by Mount Goddard; from its 13,568-foot summit virtually every major Sierra peak stands out clearly. All the early pioneers of the range had hopes of reaching this isolated viewpoint. Members of the 1864 California Geological Survey party failed, as explained earlier, but soon such illustrious names as Winchell, Solomons, Hutchinson, and LeConte graced the summit register. The latter thought the view to be "unquestionably the most extensive to be found in the Sierra." By 1912 fifty persons had reached the summit, a remarkable number considering the lengthy approach. The mountain remains a popular goal to this day. From the outlet of Wanda Lake stroll up easy terrain to the southwest to the minor ridge overlooking Davis Lake. Continue south up this low-angled ridge until it becomes feasible to work left into a shallow basin that eventually terminates atop the Goddard Divide. From this 12,400-foot pass cross tedious talus on the southern flank of Peak 13,081 until reaching the base of the summit pyramid of Mount Goddard. The final 800-foot talus slope requires stamina, not skill.

Mount Huxley

Although the view from the top of Mount Huxley is not as all-encompassing as those from the two peaks just described, its ascent proves far shorter and more challenging. The beautifully sculpted peak does offer an unparalleled view of the Mount Darwin massif. The mountain is climbed most easily from the first lakes below Wanda Lake, where several class 2–3 routes lead up the left side of the west face. Upon reaching the summit arête, turn right and scramble over to the top.

Mount Spencer

Hikers who evince no interest in climbing mountains nevertheless should consider ascending Mount Spencer. This short and easy climb leads to a viewpoint not easily forgotten. Leave the High Route at Sapphire Lake and work up into the cirque to the east. After reaching the basin's first lakes, work north up gentle terrain to the saddle just east of the mountain. A short class 2 scramble then leads to the 12,400-foot summit.

Mount Darwin

To mountaineers who collect major Sierra summits, the name Mount Darwin signifies a mandatory climb. At 13,-830 feet it is the highest crest peak between Mount Humphreys and Mount Agassiz, a distance of nearly fifteen miles. The ascent, however, is recommended only to those persons capable of negotiating complex class 3 rock. The routefinding is difficult and time-consuming, and the ascent must not be undertaken lightly. In 1895 Theodore Solomons and Ernest Bonner attempted what is now the standard ascent route, failing several hundred feet below the summit plateau. "Farther ascent," Solomons later wrote, "is barred to all human beings." His route—or a variant of it—was not completed until 1908.

Leave the High Route near the south end of Evolution Lake and climb up toward the myriad avalanche chutes visible above. The easiest route, involving much class 3 rock, is impossible to describe because of the absence of landmarks. But in general the mountaineer begins in the left-hand chutes and ends up eventually in the right-hand chutes. At last the climber reaches the summit plateau, a reminder of what the ancient Sierra looked like before the great uplifts and massive glaciation.

The actual high point of Mount Darwin is a small, delicate pinnacle curiously separated from the southeast rim of the summit plateau. Although the climbing on this spire is not particularly difficult, the exposure proves enormous, and only those adventurers familiar with airy class 3–4 rock should attempt it.

Peak 12,971

Some peaks are reached so easily from the High Route that they should not be missed. One such is Peak 12,971, a Glacier Divide summit just south of Snow-Tongue Pass. The class 2 talus ridge takes less than an hour from the pass, and the views from the top of the peak are stupendous. Mount Humphreys, less than five miles distant, stands etched unforgettably against the sky, its steep flanks plunging into barren Humphreys Basin. To the southeast rise the soaring summits of the Evolution group;

preeminent is Mount Darwin, recognized by the shimmering glacier reposing under its precipitous north face.

Mount Humphreys

Every Sierra mountaineer hopes someday to stand atop mighty Mount Humphreys. Unlike most peaks in the Sierra, this 13,986-foot colossus proves spectacular from every vantage point. And, as one might expect, such a towering formation has no truly easy route. Indeed, the final section of the standard route is steep and exposed, and though the class 4 climbing is not particularly difficult, a rope should be carried and used. The difficult section of Mount Humphreys is so short—perhaps 100 feet —and is composed of such solid rock, that its ascent seems eminently suitable for adventurous High Route mountaineers, provided, of course, there is a leader who knows how to belay properly.

The southwest base of the peak is reached easily from the High Route by any one of numerous cross-country routes across Humphreys Basin. Start up the actual peak via a conspicuous, left-diagonaling gully that slices up and across the face to the large notch seen just left of the summit pyramid. This gap marks the approximate high point reached by Joseph LeConte and Clarence Cory on their 1898 attempt. Feeling "utterly overpowered" by the steep cliffs above the notch, the two men retreated. At this stage of his mountaineering career LeConte probably was too inexperienced to appreciate two elementary facts:

frontal views distort the true steepness, and, from a distance, one cannot possibly predict the size and character of the handholds and footholds.

The first complete ascent of this route didn't take place until 1919, when climbing-party leader George Bunn seemed just as impressed as LeConte with the final tower: "A rocky depression indented the main ridge toward the summit, but this grew rapidly steeper until . . . it was so perpendicular that it leaned over backward." The Bunn party decided to investigate the route at close range, "hoping to solve each difficulty as it presented itself. . . ." By using what Bunn termed "sheer muscular power," the group attained the summit in short order.

The depression described by Bunn can be recognized immediately by the present-day climber. Scramble up this ever-steepening trough until forced to the right on narrow ledges, then climb a steep rib to the easier ground just below the summit. Most climbers will wish to break out the rope near the top of the trough and belay each other until close to the summit.

Virtually every major peak of the High Sierra is visible from Humphreys' minuscule summit. If the day is clear, the climber can discern Mount Whitney fifty miles to the south. In the opposite direction, forty miles distant, rise the distinctive outlines of Mount Ritter and Banner Peak. The precipitous dropoff on the northeast side of the peak is perhaps the single most impressive sight, for the Owens Valley, dominated by the town of Bishop, lies an unbelievable 9,800 feet below.

Pilot Knob

Pilot Knob, the symmetrical hulk five miles west of Mount Humphreys, provides another fine vantage point, one far more easily reached than its striking neighbor. The upper part of the 12,245-foot peak is a simple scramble from the prominent saddle just to the east. This gap can be reached from the High Route in less than an hour by approaching from either Mesa or Puppet lakes.

Feather Peak

One of the most rewarding summits attainable from the High Route is Feather Peak. Climbed and named in 1933 by David Brower, it is designated on the map simply as Peak 13,242. Lying three-quarters of a mile northwest of Royce Peak, the mountain can be ascended from the High Route at Feather Pass by means of its classically delineated southwest ridge. The trekker must deviate from this ridge occasionally to keep the level of difficulty down to class 3. The climbing is continuous and moderately exposed, factors which contribute to a thrilling adventure.

Seven Gables

First climbed in 1894 by Theodore Solomons and Leigh Bierce, Seven Gables long has been praised as one of the range's grandest viewpoints. Solomons himself was the first to exult about it: "I was too awed to shout. The ideas represented by such words as lovely, beautiful, wild or terrible, cold or desolate, fail to compass it. Words are puny things, and the language of description quite as impotent as the painter's brush. Roughly speaking, one might say that the sight was sublime and awful." Solomons, fascinated with the splendid austerity visible below, could "fancy several hotels—perish the thought—pitched in the glacial valley. . . . The most-used path of the many that are to lead from these Swiss-like edifices will ascend the Seven Gables, and the register in the monumental cairn built on its summit will be filled with eulogies scrawled in all languages." Mercifully, no hotels or huts presently mar the view, and the thousands of hikers who have signed the register all have traveled from campsites to do so.

Other mountaineers have been equally impressed with the view from Seven Gables. In 1898 Joseph LeConte remained on the summit for many hours, "gazing at the wonderful panorama," and in the 1921 issue of the *Sierra Club Bulletin,* Francis Farquhar listed nearly twenty prominent summits—from Mount Lyell to Mount Whitney—visible from the 13,075-foot peak.

The superlative viewpoint can be reached quite easily from the High Route. Leave the route at Ursa Lake and follow a brook downstream to its junction with the East Fork of Bear Creek. From here ascend a 1,500-foot talus slope to the prominent saddle between double-summited Seven Gables and its sharp northern satellite. A class 2 ridge then leads south to the summit.

4

Lake Country:

A typical High Sierra lake, set like a jewel amid pines and granite.

Lake Italy to Devil's Postpile

I HAVE SOMETIMES been asked what charm there can be in the higher levels of the Sierra, when the forests are gone and nothing remains that is not dead and forbidding, the bare crags and the snow-fields. To such a question the surest answer would be an evening spent in such a camp as we had that night. Such a scene!— wild, desolate, cold, forbidding, fascinating! White granite for miles, black shadows in the cañons and clefts, glistening snow, and tiny lakes sparkling in the moonlight; jagged, fantastic peaks and pinnacles with alpine intensity of light and shadow, and masses of ice and snow clinging to the gentler slopes. And withal the intense quiet and loneliness of the place, a seeming new world on a new planet where man and his works are as nothing. The thrill of it all comes even now, though months have passed, and will remain through the years to come.

Lincoln Hutchinson,
describing the timberline country
near Cotton Lake.
From the February 1903 issue
of the *Sierra Club Bulletin*.

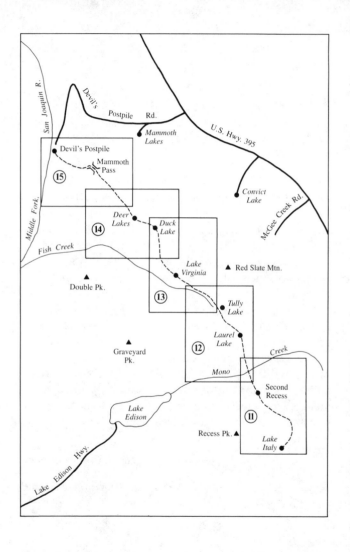

E VEN THOUGH the central portion of the High Route negotiates two major east-west ridges—the Mono and Silver divides—it still remains the easiest of the five segments. Entailing only a few sections more challenging than class 2, the segment extending from Lake Italy northward to Devil's Postpile traverses a magnificent landscape blessed with an inordinate share of gentle granite slabs and flower-strewn meadowlands. True, hikers must clamber over talus blocks from time to time, but such terrain rarely persists more than a few hundred yards.

Leaving Lake Italy behind, the backpacker ascends remarkably pleasant slabs to Gabbot Pass, the last location above 12,000 feet on the High Route. Soon the hiker strolls through the Second Recess, where a dense, coniferous forest comprises the most luxuriant setting since LeConte Canyon. Crossing Mono Creek at 8,500 feet, the High Route immediately surmounts the formidable north wall of the canyon. Once this obstacle is overcome, the hiker winds up delightful countryside to the Silver Divide, the watershed boundary between the South and Middle forks of the San Joaquin River. Not far north of here, the route follows the John Muir Trail for a few miles in order to circumvent a rugged, undistinguished section closer to the crest. The final portion of this segment of the High Route follows the main crestline along Mammoth Crest before dropping precipitously to the Middle Fork at Devil's Postpile.

Since the countryside surrounding both the Mono and Silver divides appears to be more rugged than it actually is, the early explorers shunned the main crest and its two great spurs in favor of the less complex country to the west, where the South Fork of the San Joaquin River afforded an obvious thoroughfare toward the prominent peaks of the Evolution group and the Goddard Divide. Nevertheless, the main watersheds of the region became fairly well known during the last one-third of the nineteenth century. In 1864 members of the California Geological Survey crossed the range at Mono Pass and descended Mono Creek westward. But this group reached only one minor summit, and the map that resulted from their labors displayed numerous blank areas. Thirty-one years later, Theodore Solomons spent several days in the environs of Mono Creek, exploring the curious u-shaped trenches he called "recesses." Like his predecessors, Solomons avoided the summits, preferring instead to travel along the many branches of the San Joaquin.

At last, during the ten-year-period from 1898 to 1908, the heart of the area became thoroughly known. Joseph

LeConte and James Hutchinson, those ubiquitous Sierra explorers, ascended the region's highest summits, from which they named features and mapped the countryside. Three passes, now integral components of the High Route, first were visited by one or both of these pioneers. Bighorn and Shout-of-Relief passes were crossed by Hutchinson in 1902, a few hours after he and two companions had made the first ascent of nearby Red and White Mountain. Gabbot Pass, the key to crossing the upper Mono Divide, was reached by Hutchinson and LeConte in 1908; the latter noted that the pass would provide "a great cut-off in the High Mountain Route," which at that time circumvented the Mono Divide in the lowlands far to the west.

After the pioneers had examined every cirque and most mountaintops, the area became frequented by curious hikers who wished to see the scenery so extolled by LeConte, Hutchinson, and their cohorts. These newcomers climbed the minor peaks, fished the creeks that churn tumultuously down the enormous canyons, and camped beside the numerous—and particularly lovely—lakes dotting the landscape in every direction.

Although the High Route wends its way past hundreds of magnificent lakes during its 195-mile journey, this central segment seems to harbor a disproportionate share of the most attractive ones. Indeed, several of these lakes fulfill all the prerequisites for entering a "perfect mountain lake" contest. Such a lake displays a few apparently bottomless deeps where venerable trout—traditionally uncatchable—arrogantly flash their brilliant colors. Nearby, superimposed on a shallow underwater bench, myriad fingerlings dart with unfathomable alacrity across current-sculpted sand. Multicolored granite cliffs plunge dramatically into the blue; a hundred feet away, however, lush meadows border sandy beaches. Both the inlet and the outlet streams vie for attention, and in the distance, beyond the lakeshore's wonderfully twisted pines, serrated peaks dominate the horizon.

Which lake is the most sublime in this region? Is it Lower Mills Creek Lake, Laurel Lake, or one of the lovely ponds dotting the basin north of Shout-of-Relief Pass? Could the winner be the largest of the Deer Lakes? Or might it be some unnamed body of water a few hundred yards from the High Route, a place visited by only a handful of adventurers? Travelers probably will agree that no single lake wins the contest; many share first place.

Approaches

Lake Italy, the southern terminus of this segment of the High Route, can be reached from the east via the Italy Pass Trail. This ten-mile path, involving an elevation gain of nearly 5,000 feet, begins just below the Pine Creek Tungsten Mill, a mining complex reached by a paved road leaving U.S. Highway 395 north of Bishop.

Lake Italy also can be reached from the western flank of the Sierra. Several miles south of the dam at Lake

Edison, a spur road leaves the main highway and winds east a few miles to the Bear Diversion Dam. From here a trail parallels Bear Creek until joining the John Muir Trail at Kip Camp. Follow this path south a few miles, then turn east along the trail leading up the Hilgard Branch of Bear Creek. Lake Italy is reached in half a dozen miles; the total trail distance from the roadhead is just over fifteen miles.

The High Route can be intersected quite easily where it crosses Mono Creek. Originating from the west end of Lake Edison, a well-traveled trail proceeds along the reservoir, parallels Mono Creek, and finally meets the High Route opposite the Second Recess. The trail from the east begins near Rock Creek Lake, climbs over the Sierra crest at Mono Pass, and descends Mono Creek until meeting the High Route at the point where it begins climbing the canyon wall north toward Laurel Lake. Each of these approaches is approximately eleven miles in length.

Hikers who wish to join the High Route midway along this central segment can do so via the McGee Pass Trail. This scenic path crosses the Sierra crest just south of lofty Red Slate Mountain and meets the High Route at Horse Heaven, a handsome meadow at the 9,600-foot level of Fish Creek.

Devil's Postpile, the northern terminus of this portion of the High Route, is reached easily by road from the Mammoth Lakes region. See the "Approaches" section of Chapter 5 for details.

The longest loop trip possible in this segment is a fairly obvious one: follow the High Route all the way to Devil's Postpile, then return via the John Muir Trail.

Another loop trip, shorter but more challenging than the preceding one, should appeal to hardy hikers who leave their cars near the Pine Creek Tungsten Mill. After following the High Route to the lake-dotted basin north of Shout-of-Relief Pass, wander north a few miles and intersect the McGee Pass Trail. Take this path east over the crest to Big McGee Lake, then work south over Hopkins Pass, a straightforward class 2 saddle. After descending easy terrain alongside Hopkins Creek, follow the trail over Mono Pass into Little Lakes Valley. At this point, pick up the path that crosses Morgan Pass and ends at the tungsten mill.

The High Route

Lake Italy to Second Recess

Standing at the outlet of Lake Italy, the High Route backpacker immediately faces a dilemma: which side of the two-mile-long lake offers the easiest method of reaching Gabbot Pass? In 1908 the three pioneers who first climbed nearby Mount Abbot faced the same problem, and—with a fifty-fifty chance of choosing the easiest side —made the wrong decision. Invisible from the outlet, a half-mile-long section far along the lake's southern shore contains enormous, unstable blocks of granite; although this side is passable, it cannot be recommended. LeConte, Hutchinson, and McDuffie returned from their climb via the northern shore; this proved trivial by comparison and is now the standard route around the lake.

Thus forewarned, the hiker should follow the northern shore of the huge lake until reaching its eastern end, where a long, surprisingly gentle slope rises to the north. Aim for Gabbot Pass, the conspicuous saddle separating massive Mount Gabb from delicate Mount Abbot. The panorama from the 12,250-foot pass proves somewhat disappointing for such an elevated vantage point, for one is hemmed in by the nearby peaks. But to the south, beyond the west shoulder of Mount Julius Caesar, towers impressive, flat-topped Feather Peak, a familiar friend to those hikers who have completed the previous segment of the High Route. To the north, thirty-one miles distant, rise the twin sentinels that so dominate the northern High Sierra: Mount Ritter and Banner Peak.

The High Route in the vicinity of Gabbot Pass is cursed with an inordinate number of "ducks," those piles of rock constructed by well-intentioned hikers who imagine they are the only ones capable of finding the easiest route. These ducks, unnecessary and often misleading, spoil the sense of adventure for hikers who believe, however falsely, that they are explorers wandering across uncharted lands. It must be admitted that ducks have been around a long time; the first mention of the annoying markers in the

Sierra Club Bulletin occurs in the June 1905 issue. Four years later, in the same journal, a brief controversy flared regarding the etymology of the word "duck." The savants finally agreed that it derived from "duckstone," a game popular in nineteenth-century England. The object of this rather mindless game was to knock off, from a distance, a small stone—the duck—that had been placed atop a larger one. Present-day High Route hikers should play this game whenever possible, until all existing ducks have vanished.

Drop down from Gabbot Pass into a gently angled valley that winds through stable talus interspersed with sandy flats. After about half a mile the hiker reaches a shallow tarn just below the terminal moraine of the inconspicuous "rock" glacier on the north side of Mount Gabb. Finding the easiest way during the next mile requires some careful routefinding. When just below the tarn, bear slightly right and descend alongside a stream as it courses down a wide slot. After a short distance leave the creek and diagonal over to a small, sandy saddle on the right. From here, pick up a rudimentary path that drops down a precipitous slope into a barren valley. Walk down this path for a few hundred yards to a fine viewpoint. At this point the traveler might be tempted to drop straight down to Upper Mills Creek Lake, visible below. This is indeed possible, but the easier route once again veers to the right, crossing a short, jumbled section of talus, to another barren valley. This valley eventually debouches into the meadowlands near the tarns below Upper Mills Creek Lake.

From the meadows below Upper Mills Creek Lake, follow a distinct path down the east side of the prominent creek, reaching timberline at exquisite Lower Mills Creek Lake. The region just below the lake's outlet fulfills all expectations of what a Sierra landscape should include. The creek slithers down glacier-polished slabs, drops into deep pools, then winds silently through serpentine channels etched into fragile meadows dotted with wildflowers. Stands of exotically twisted pines—some remarkably large for the elevation—are scattered across the meadowlands. In the background the steplike profile of Mount Abbot dominates the scene, especially at sundown, when for a few minutes it alone retains the alpenglow shared earlier by the other great peaks.

At some juncture the hiker must bid farewell to this idyllic place where the elements are so gracefully balanced. A path—faint and difficult to locate at times—descends the north side of Mills Creek, keeping some distance from it. After about a mile the traveler arrives at the brink of an exceptionally steep slope that falls into the striking glacial canyon known as the Second Recess. The path, by now quite distinct, zigzags down this brushy, scree-covered hillside.

During this descent the hiker can enjoy an unusual Sierra sight. Across the Second Recess, and about one mile distant, is a gigantic, heart-shaped hole in a steep cliff.

So incongruous is this feature that the mind struggles to explain it. Perhaps it is a gouge left after a massive rockfall —no, it is too deep. Perhaps it is a cave—but, no, caves don't occur in granite. All one can say is that it is a mysterious feature.

Second Recess to Bighorn Pass

The dense forest covering the floor of the Second Recess should delight High Route trekkers, for it is the most luxuriant since the floor of LeConte Canyon. Enormous western white pines, recognized by their elongated cones, tower amid the more predominant lodgepole pines. The nearby mountains for once are overshadowed by the forest. A pleasant path winds down the valley, remaining close to a crystal-clear brook that meanders through the trees and meadows.

After a mile and a half of strolling through this tranquil valley, the hiker arrives at the slope that falls off into the canyon of Mono Creek. Here the observant traveler can easily absorb an elemental lesson in geology. The Second Recess, like its three neighboring recesses, is known as a hanging valley, a common feature of glaciated mountains. After a glacier has scoured a major valley, the side valleys are necessarily left suspended far above the floor of the main canyon. Thus, they terminate rather abruptly, though this depends on their size and subsequent erosion. The hiker who descends from the Second Recess is at one moment striding along the floor of a side valley and at the next zigzagging down the steep flank of a main valley. Hanging valleys occur throughout the Sierra, but the four Mono Recesses are prime examples of the genre, largely because of their enormous size and classic U shape.

The trail next descends through a stately forest of red firs, trees not seen on the High Route since the environs of Kings Canyon. The appearance of this ramrod-straight evergreen means that the hiker has reached the "low Sierra," for *Abies magnifica* rarely occurs above the 9,500-foot level. Cross Mono Creek on any of several fallen-log bridges and join the Mono Pass Trail on the opposite side. Follow it upstream for about half a mile until reaching a trail junction 100 feet west of Laurel Creek. An inconspicuous sign informs the traveler that the path heading north up the slope leads to Laurel Lake.

As if to make up for the embarrassingly low elevation, the Laurel Lake Trail attacks the steep hillside with a vengeance. Eschewing switchbacks, the poorly maintained path cuts more or less straight up through dense thickets of manzanita. If the day is hot, the steepness, low elevation, and lack of shade trees make for a somewhat unpleasant hour's hike. Take heart, however, for at the 9,300-foot level a few noble specimens of Jeffrey pine provide cool resting places where the traveler can gaze across Mono Creek toward the classic shape of the Second Recess. Another interesting feature lies just left of the entrance to the recess, in line with massive Mount Gabb. A pale green swath slicing down the darker green of the forest indicates that an avalanche raked this slope not long ago, destroying every pine in its path. Quaking aspens now have replaced the pines, adding a welcome variation to the flora.

At last the path levels off and draws close to placid Laurel Creek, a gratifying sight to the thirsty traveler. Continue along the west bank of the creek until reaching a meadow—or bog, depending on the season—at 9,700 feet. Cross the creek here and follow a faint path through fine-looking stands of lodgepole pines. After surmounting a short headwall, the path meanders up a pleasant valley that eventually ends at Laurel Lake, a secluded timberline pond.

Leave this body of water near the two massive granite blocks adorning its northwest shore and ascend precipitous, grassy slopes that lead upward 900 feet to Bighorn Pass, the 11,250-foot saddle immediately east of Rosy Finch Lake. The nomenclature in this region is historically interesting. In July 1902, James Hutchinson, his brother Lincoln, and Charles Noble decided to cross this gap while returning to their camp near Cotton Lake. East of the pass, they were surprised to spy a band of twenty mountain sheep, an animal the men had thought long since extinct. Tired after their first ascent of nearby Red and White Mountain, the men still managed to follow two of the agile, inquisitive beasts to the very crest of the ridge, where they vanished. The men decided to commemorate the incident by naming the lake below after the mountain sheep. But in later years their name inexplicably was transferred to the next lake to the west, and the deep, rockbound body of water directly below the pass is known today as Rosy Finch Lake. But the pass itself should bear a name that is historically valid, even if the animals haven't traveled over the pass for many decades.

The view from Bighorn Pass is spectacular. Just beyond Rosy Finch Lake rises the sharp silhouette of Mount Izaak Walton. Historian Francis Farquhar suggested this name in 1919 to memorialize the man "to whom all fishermen and lovers of good literature are indebted for *The Compleat Angler.*" Seven miles to the south of Bighorn Pass lie the four distinctive peaks that guard the upper reaches of the glacier-scooped Second Recess: Mount Abbot, huge Mount Gabb, Mount Hilgard, and truncated Recess Peak.

Bighorn Pass to Tully Hole

From Bighorn Pass the traveler should study the next section of the High Route, for the routefinding is a bit tricky. The next objective, a broad saddle two-thirds of a mile to the northwest, rises only a few hundred feet higher than Bighorn Pass, yet there is no easy way to contour across the labyrinthine countryside beneath the imposing cliffs of Peak 12,238 and its satellites. Therefore, drop down about seventy-five vertical feet from the pass, then begin clambering across rocky outcrops and short stretches of talus. Contour whenever possible, but be prepared for minor climbs and descents. There are no technical difficulties whatsoever, and the traverse from pass to pass should consume less than one hour.

When the exhausted first ascenders of Red and White Mountain reached this pass and scrutinized the gentle terrain on the opposite side, they let out a "shout of relief," according to Lincoln Hutchinson. It seems fitting that the name of this gap on the Silver Divide commemorate the emotions of the three pioneers—thus, I have termed it Shout-of-Relief Pass. The name seems doubly appropriate for this High Route pass, since the next twenty-five miles of the route pose few problems for the hiker. North of this divide, the traveler enters a region distinguished by its gentleness; rugged country will be encountered next at Nancy Pass, the gateway to the Ritter Range.

Looking north from Shout-of-Relief Pass, the traveler gazes across hundreds of square miles of mountainous terrain. Mount Ritter and Banner Peak, last seen from Gabbot Pass, now loom much more prominently; these easily recognizable masses are but two dozen miles distant. Closer to the viewer rise the clusters of unnamed summits that make up the crest region south of Mammoth Mountain. If these metamorphic hulks lack the shapeliness of other peaks in the range, at least they are far more colorful in appearance. Reds, browns, purples, buffs—all charm the jaded High Route walker accustomed to monotonously hued granite.

The pleasant and gently angled terrain dropping north

of Shout-of-Relief Pass enables the hiker to reach, in short order, a medium-sized basin dotted with minuscule ponds and isolated clumps of conifers. This verdant parkland, located just one-half mile from a major trail, remains remarkably untrammeled, and hikers who stroll west under the shoulder of Peak 11,411 toward Cotton Lake easily might envision themselves traversing meadows untrodden by human feet.

Because of its relative luxuriance, this parkland attracts a singularly complete cross-section of the breeding birds of the Sierra timberline country. Dark-eyed juncos, easily recognized by their small size and jet black heads, are the birds most commonly encountered, but patient observers will see, even without binoculars, numerous other species, some of which are described below.

Mountain bluebirds often are spotted; they radiate an ethereal light blue glow that contrasts vividly with the weathered wood surrounding the entrance to their nests, old woodpecker holes in dead pine snags. Yellow-rumped warblers, distinguished by the bright yellow feathers ornamenting various parts of their bodies, flit restlessly among the pines, occasionally bursting into the sky to snare insects in a delightfully acrobatic fashion. Clark's nutcrackers, the noisiest residents of timberline country, flash bold patches of black, gray, and white as they hurtle from one treetop to another during their relentless quest for pine nuts.

The sight of a Hammond's flycatcher, a fairly drab

denizen of the treetops, excites the serious birdwatcher, for this species proves difficult to identify unless seen in its preferred breeding habitat, the subalpine wilderness. Ralph Hoffmann, author of *Birds of the Pacific States,* relates a wry anecdote in which this tiny bird plays a role: "When Theodore Roosevelt first met John Muir, it is reported that his first question was, 'How can one tell the Hammond from the Wright Flycatcher?' It is doubtful whether any future President of the United States will have the slightest interest in the problem."

After leaving this delightful outdoor aviary, wander over past Cotton Lake to the dropoff overlooking Izaak Walton Lake, a narrow body of water reposing in a handsome setting. After working down slabs and gullies, circle the lake to its outlet and descend the tree-covered benches bordering the frenzied stream below. After a descent of about 450 feet, the hiker will meet Fish Creek at the upper edge of Horse Heaven, a swampy meadow at the 9,700-foot level. Join the McGee Pass Trail on the opposite bank of the creek and stroll down the spectacular canyon below.

The hiker shortly encounters another enormous meadow; here, at Tully Hole, the John Muir Trail is reached. Not since Evolution Lake—some fifty trail miles to the south—has the High Route followed this famous path. But because of the complex and unattractive country near the Sierra crest, the next six miles of the High Route are concomitant with the John Muir Trail. This scarcely qualifies as a hardship, however, for the countryside remains beautiful.

Tully Hole to Deer Lakes

North of the Tully Hole junction, the trail immediately assails the steep wall of Fish Creek Canyon by means of marvelously constructed switchbacks. Soon after crossing a wooded saddle, the traveler reaches Lake Virginia, an oblong lake situated on a wide bench overlooking Cascade Valley, some 1,800 feet below.

Lovely Purple Lake is the next major landmark along the route. Shortly after passing this feature, the well-graded trail curves around the southern and western flanks of Peak 11,348. During this long traverse the hiker enjoys a continuously interesting view of not only Cascade Valley but the soaring peaks that make up the northwestern end of the Silver Divide.

The traveler soon reaches the marked turnoff to Duck Lake; leave the John Muir Trail here and zigzag up the incline to the north. Duck Lake, the largest body of water attained by the High Route so far, makes its appearance at last. The lake probably was named after the waterfowl that, in the late season, occasionally pause here during their migratory journey to the south.

From the lake's outlet the trail immediately begins climbing the hillside to the north. Continue for one mile to a wooded gap at 10,800 feet. Here, at Duck Pass, the High Route meets the Sierra crest for the first time. Since this portion of the divide is relatively gentle, the saddle does not offer the hiker a very satisfactory panorama. Although Mount Ritter and Banner Peak rise prominently to the north, few other significant peaks can be identified.

The lackluster view, however, is partially offset by a local attraction. On the whitebark-covered acres west of the pass, and just below the ridgeline, the traveler will discover thousands of obsidian chips, a sure sign that Indians once used this site to fashion their arrowheads.

Leave Duck Pass and follow the Sierra crest west up a gentle hillside. After a short distance the hiker can identify a portion of huge Mono Lake, some twenty-five miles distant. "The lonely tenant of the loneliest spot on earth," Mark Twain once called it. The extremely saline body of water remains relatively unknown a hundred years later, a fact that, ironically, may hasten its demise. Much of the water that formerly poured into the lake from the mountains is now diverted to Los Angeles to help meet the insatiable needs of that burgeoning metropolis. Consequently, the lake's level is dropping alarmingly fast, and if the public does not demand a stop to this practice, the basin will one day become an enormous alkaline wasteland, devoid of life. No longer will visitors be entranced by the sight of hundreds of thousands of eared grebes who pause each autumn during migration. No longer will California gulls brighten the sky around moonlike Negit Island, their nesting grounds for untold milleniums.

With this reminder of man's folly constantly in sight, continue along the fairly level main crest until reaching the low saddle just to the right of craggy Peak 11,647. The view to the south from this 11,200-foot pass proves so superior to that from Duck Pass that it is hard to believe the latter lies only half a mile away and 400 feet lower. Although the upper portions of both Red Slate Mountain and Red and White Mountain are visible, the prime view is of the Mount Abbot group and Seven Gables; both massifs loom prominently.

A surprise awaits the viewer who turns to the north, for beyond the pass lies an extensive, but shallow, basin, not at all what one would expect on the usually precipitous eastern flank of the Sierra. The only long-distance view to the north is of the Clark Range, a major ridge near Yosemite Valley. In line with this isolated chain of peaks, and only a quarter of a mile distant, the hiker can distinguish another low gap on the Sierra crest. Cross the sand-covered basin to this saddle, then descend a gentle slope west for about 100 feet. There, at an abrupt dropoff, is a splendid view of the three Deer Lakes in their pleasant, inviting setting.

A good path winds down the steep talus slope, and in a few minutes the hiker arrives at the scree-covered benches above the uppermost Deer Lake. Leave the faint path near here and wander over hill and dale to the northernmost Deer Lake, an exquisite body of water ringed by slabs and meadows.

Deer Lakes to Mammoth Pass

Head west a few hundred feet from this lake and join the Deer Creek Trail as it assaults the hillside to the north in a rudely direct manner. After a climb of about 400 vertical feet, the traveler approaches the main Sierra crest yet again. Here, along what is called Mammoth Crest, the trail begins contouring just below the ridgeline. At one point the trail passes a "window" in the crest, and from there the viewer can gaze straight down into the populated valley of Mammoth Creek; this marks the first sign of civilization along the High Route thus far.

The panorama from Mammoth Crest rivals any of the entire High Route. So isolated and high is this airy ridge that the viewer has the impression of staring at the landscape from an airplane. To the south, Mount Hilgard and its distinctive, flat-topped neighbor, Recess Peak, can be seen. Seven Gables, as always, rises spectacularly against the skyline. To its right, displaying a sheer northern escarpment, is Mount Hooper, the guardian of the Selden Pass region.

It is to the north, however, that the panorama outdoes itself. The entire Clark Range is visible, as is the dark and sinister Ritter Range. To the left of the spires comprising the Minarets—and far beyond them—rises the massive white pyramid called Foerster Peak; the traveler later will cross the pass just to its left as the High Route enters Yosemite National Park. Framed perfectly in the Ritter-

Banner saddle is lofty Mount Lyell, nineteen miles distant. Farther right, the viewer can identify Donohue Peak by the parallel avalanche chutes on its south face. Closer at hand is bleak Mammoth Mountain; its blockhouselike summit building is the only indication of the superlative ski area on the opposite side.

Soon after leaving the highest part of Mammoth Crest, the hiker begins a gradual descent through a sparse white-bark-pine forest. Later, on an extensive plateau, pictur-esque whitebark snags, along with healthy specimens, line the indistinct main crest like sentinels guarding against invaders from the west. The mountains on all sides seem disembodied, for their lower ramparts are hidden beneath the rim of the plateau. Because of the "floating" moun-tains and the primordial foreground, a mystical quality pervades this plateau, and it seems incomprehensible that one is standing atop the Sierra crest.

Follow the crestline north for another mile or so, enter-ing along the way a zone of twisted, red lava, extremely young by geological standards. Finally, at a small knoll, the Deer Creek Trail drops inconspicuously toward Mam-moth Lakes. The High Route continues along the crest, passing several notches that overlook the by-now sheer east side of the range. After about half a mile, the traveler reaches the top of the steep dropoff overlooking Mam-moth Pass, that vast gap in the main crest south of Mam-moth Mountain. Steep cliffs lie below this point, so diagonal down west to the obvious sandy saddle just east of Peak 10,005. Don't waste time looking for the trail indicated on the topo map, for it does not exist, at least not in any maintained fashion. This fact proves to be no problem when going downhill, for the hiker simply can plow down the pumice-filled gully that debouches onto Mammoth Pass. The general unpleasantness of this short section is partially offset by the appearance of the delicate mountain hemlock, which in a few hundred feet almost totally usurps the whitebark pines. This graceful conifer, generally absent from the southern Sierra, will be seen quite often on the remainder of the High Route.

Mammoth Pass to Devil's Postpile

The terrain levels out eventually, and the traveler should continue north across wide Mammoth Pass through a dense forest of lodgepole pines. Upon encountering a trail, step across it and strike north cross-country for about 400 yards to a second trail, which, judging by its well-worn appearance, is more heavily traveled than the first. Here, at 9,300 feet, is a tranquil area that almost demands that the traveler pause and contemplate the surroundings.

Although Mammoth Pass forms the lowest spot on the entire High Sierra crest, its more interesting attribute concerns its geology. Near here, eons ago, basalt surged forth from a vent and plunged into the canyon of the Middle Fork of the San Joaquin River. As explained in the following chapter, one remnant of this flow is known today as Devil's Postpile. Much more visible than the basalt, however, is the layer of pumice that blankets the entire Mammoth Pass region. Although this pumice forms only a veneer in most locations, near the pass it is estimated to be nearly 1,000 feet thick. The steam-shredded bits of siliceous lava, astonishingly light and delicate, were carried here by the wind following the explosions of the numerous small volcanoes south of Mono Lake.

During heavy rainstorms this pumice floats eerily in the depression of the trail, causing travelers to question their eyesight at times. More frequently, however, the pumice simply annoys the hiker, for it is difficult to move efficiently through the loose, airy material. High Route trekkers become immediately aware of this fact as they head west on the trail as it begins its 1,700-foot descent to the Middle Fork.

After about one-and-a-half miles—during which time the traveler has entered a fine stand of red firs—the John Muir Trail is encountered. After another mile or so this trail levels out on the valley floor; at 7,600 feet, this is the lowest elevation reached by the entire High Route, except for its two end points.

The hiker then follows the John Muir Trail as it winds

on a circuitous route toward nearby Devil's Postpile, the northern terminus of this segment of the High Route. Red's Meadow, with its store and ranger station, lies close by for those travelers in need of amenities or assistance.

Reversing the Route

Southbound travelers on this segment of the High Route encounter their first routefinding dilemma at Mammoth Pass, where they must locate the correct gully leading up onto Mammoth Crest. Because the flat acres constituting Mammoth Pass are blanketed with a dense stand of lodgepole pines, it proves somewhat difficult to discover a break from which to peer south. But after locating such a gap, the traveler can see, about half a mile distant, a massive, rocky bluff directly on the Sierra crest. To its right is a sandy saddle with a wide, tree-covered gully dropping from it. (On the map this gully is located directly east of Peak 10,005. The trail shown on the map does not exist.) Ascend the tedious, sandy slopes leading to the saddle, then work up the incline on the left. Soon the hiker will be striding south along Mammoth Crest.

Follow the trail along Mammoth Crest until, after several miles, it drops abruptly to the northernmost of the Deer Lakes. Leave the trail here and work east across gentle terrain until nearly at the southeastern Deer Lake;

from there the traveler can spot, close at hand to the east, a conspicuous gap in the Sierra crest. A rough path zig-zags up 250 feet to this 11,200-foot pass.

The hiker does not remain on the eastern side of the Sierra for long. Work east across a sand-covered flat for one-quarter of a mile to a prominent saddle that barely rises above the level of the basin. From here the traveler can easily study the gentle terrain leading down and across to Duck Pass.

Hikers should encounter no further routefinding problems until approaching the Silver Divide. The first place that may prove perplexing occurs a mile or so after leaving the John Muir Trail. The hiker must leave the McGee Pass Trail near the far end of the pleasant meadow known as Horse Heaven and ascend the slope alongside the stream draining Izaak Walton Lake. After passing around this narrow body of water, turn hard left and surmount a short headwall to the bench on which Cotton Lake reposes. From here contour east around the shoulder of Peak 11,411 until reaching a tree-covered basin containing numerous lakes.

From the basin, work southeast toward Shout-of-Relief Pass, the gentle saddle immediately to the right of conspicuous Peak 12,238. (Avoid heading straight south from the lake basin; this route leads to a pass overlooking Bighorn Lake.) From Shout-of-Relief Pass the next mile of the High Route is visible. Contour southeast, occasionally moving up or down, underneath the spectacular cliff band shooting southeast from Peak 12,238. Bighorn Pass is the highest feasible crossing point along this ridge.

Much farther south, near the end of this segment of the High Route, the traveler comes across another possible routefinding problem: the north side of Gabbot Pass. From the large tarn just below Upper Mills Creek Lake, the hiker will notice several rounded hillocks more or less in line with Gabbot Pass, the obvious gap to the right of lofty Mount Abbot. The easiest route to this saddle follows crude paths hidden in shallow valleys on the far left side of the hillocks. The path fades as the traveler approaches the saddle, but by this time the route is more than obvious.

Alternate Routes

Because of the relative ease of this segment of the High Route, only one alternate route needs to be mentioned here. This alternate—which appears, upon studying the map, to be more practical than the High Route—begins at Laurel Lake. Head northeast up the hillside to meet Grinnell Lake, then proceed up rocky slopes to the 11,600-foot pass immediately west of Red and White Mountain. It is now possible to descend slate-covered slopes to the meadowlands surrounding Tully Lake. This alternate, long considered to be the standard cross-country route across the Silver Divide, proves less efficient than the High Route for three reasons: it requires an extra elevation gain; it involves traversing large sections of loose slate; and, because of its geographical setting, it retains snow until late in the season.

Mountaineering en Route

Peaks around Lake Italy

Centrally located Lake Italy provides a good starting point for several significant summits. Monolithic Mount Hilgard can be climbed in a few hours from the lake's outlet. Mount Julius Caesar, with its striking view of well-named Lake Italy, can be reached via the loose class 2 slopes that rise above Italy Pass. Bear Creek Spire can be ascended from the head of the lake: hike up seemingly endless talus to the class 3 summit rocks, which are best approached from the north.

Mount Gabb

Gabbot Pass is the standard departure point for climbing the two peaks that give the pass its name. The northeast ridge of Mount Gabb offers the mountaineer a straightforward class 3 ascent. Instead of slavishly following the ridge, wander away from it when confronted by steep sections.

Mount Abbot

As evidenced by the following statistic, early Sierra Club members were entranced by Mount Abbot: of the thirty-eight persons who signed the summit register between 1908 and 1930, all but two were members of that then-small organization. During the following half-century, of course, that ratio was not maintained, and hundreds of mountaineers with other affiliations—or none at all—have stood atop the region's highest summit. From Gabbot Pass the route is fairly clear. Ascend a talus slope over to a wide chute on the right side of the steep buttress that diagonals down from the summit. The 200-foot cliff rising above the head of the chute provides the main challenge of the route. The steep wall can be surmounted in various places; the easiest route is class 3. Once the cliff has been climbed, the top is reached by a short stroll across the surprisingly extensive summit plateau.

Red and White Mountain

Rising from the junction of the Silver Divide with the Sierra crest, Red and White Mountain offers an interesting climb capped by a superb viewpoint. The 12,850-foot summit first was reached in 1902 by the Hutchinson brothers and Charles Noble. As the victorious trio stood at the top, they tried to conjure up a "less clumsy and more euphonious" name than "Red-and-White Peak," the name bestowed by Theodore Solomons eight years earlier. Although the men knew that first-ascenders traditionally could name or rename the peaks they climbed, they finally decided to retain the old name since it was "peculiarly descriptive of the great peak of red slate fantastically streaked with seams of white granite." (By the time Norman Clyde made the second ascent twenty-six years later, "Peak" had become "Mountain"; mapmakers later dropped the hyphens.)

The summit can be reached by either of two routes, both of which leave the High Route at Laurel Lake. The first follows the upper part of the original ascent route: walk up talus to the pass between the mountain and Peak 12,238, then scramble up the serrated class 3 ridge to the top. The exposure on the upper ridge proves impressive, and a few places call for extra caution. First-ascender Lincoln Hutchinson recalled one of these spots in an article in the *Sierra Club Bulletin:* "Midway[up] the worst portion of this knife-edge we suddenly came to a huge block of slate set squarely athwart our course. Our route seemed absolutely blocked to any animal without wings, and for a few moments failure stared us in the face." But the intrepid pioneers soon solved the problem, as will the present-day mountaineer who recognizes this particular obstacle.

The second route on Red and White Mountain follows the route descended by the 1902 first-ascent party: climb the conspicuous class 2 chute that rises above Little Grinnell Lake.

Red Slate Mountain

The gigantic red pyramid known as Red Slate Mountain totally dominates its surroundings: at 13,163 feet it is the highest crest peak in many miles. Indeed, to the north, there is no higher peak in the remaining sixty miles of the High Sierra, and to the south, the serpentine crest does not pierce the 13,000-foot level once again until it rises at the Mount Abbot group, some eight miles distant. The panorama from this colorful peak encompasses a vast region, and climbers familiar with the shapes of major Sierra peaks will be able to identify dozens of them in the seventy-mile stretch of wilderness lying between Mount Conness and Mount Goddard. The High Route traveler can climb this significant peak from the vicinity of Cotton Lake. Because of loose rock and a lack of challenging sections, the ascent is not particularly enjoyable, and prospective climbers might heed the words of Joseph LeConte, one of the first-ascenders: "The jagged fragments of slate are even more trying to the patience than to the shoes."

Peak 11,348

A popular goal of day-hikers based at Mammoth Lakes, Peak 11,348 certainly is worth the ten-minute effort it takes to climb it from the High Route. This inconspicuous mountain, located on Mammoth Crest midway between Duck and Mammoth passes, provides a sterling panorama of the Mammoth Lakes region and the Ritter Range.

5

Headwaters Country:

Clyde Minaret and its glacier tower above the High Route at Iceberg Lake.

Devil's Postpile
to Tuolumne Meadows

NOW CAME THE solemn, silent evening. Long, blue,
spiky shadows crept out across the snow-fields, while a
rosy glow, at first scarce discernible, gradually
deepened and suffused every mountain-top, flushing the
glaciers and the harsh crags above them. This was the
alpenglow, to me one of the most impressive of all the
terrestrial manifestations of God. At the touch of this
divine light, the mountains seemed to kindle to a rapt,
religious consciousness, and stood hushed and waiting
like devout worshippers. Just before the alpenglow
began to fade, two crimson clouds came streaming
across the summit like wings of flame, rendering the
sublime scene yet more impressive; then came darkness
and the stars.

John Muir, describing the
arrival of nightfall at his
camp below Mount Ritter. From
The Mountains of California.

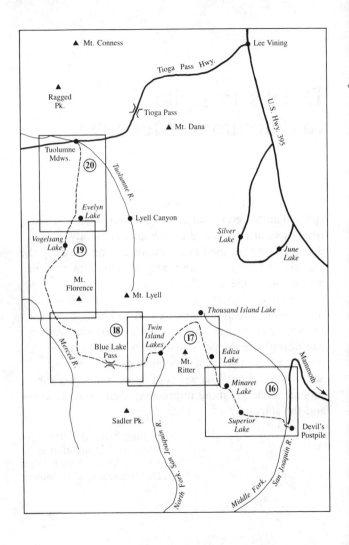

- ▲ Mt. Conness
- Lee Vining
- Tioga Pass Hwy.
- ▲ Ragged Pk.
- Tioga Pass
- ▲ Mt. Dana
- U.S. Hwy. 395
- Tuolumne Mdws.
- (20)
- Tuolumne R.
- *Evelyn Lake*
- Lyell Canyon
- *Silver Lake*
- *Vogelsang Lake*
- (19)
- June Lake
- ▲ Mt. Florence
- ▲ Mt. Lyell
- Thousand Island Lake
- Merced R.
- (18)
- *Twin Island Lakes*
- (17)
- ▲ Mt. Ritter
- *Ediza Lake*
- Blue Lake Pass
- Mammoth
- *Minaret Lake*
- (16)
- ▲ Sadler Pk.
- *Superior Lake*
- Devil's Postpile
- North Fork, San Joaquin R.
- Middle Fork, San Joaquin R.

THE HIGH ROUTE traveler well may become uneasy when surrounded by the multitudes of tourists and backpackers who cluster around the road's end near Devil's Postpile. Fortunately, he or she soon will be alone again, wandering through the spectacular wilderness that surrounds the headwaters of four major Sierra rivers: the Middle and North forks of the San Joaquin, the Merced, and the Tuolumne.

For the first few days of this segment of the High Route, the hiker traverses the sublime country lying just beneath the glacier-clad faces of the Minarets and the twin sentinels of the northern High Sierra, Mount Ritter and Banner Peak. Fishermen, climbers, and families long ago discovered the delights of this easily accessible flank of the Ritter Range, and in August numerous people camp in the most popular locations. The majority of these wilderness lovers stick closely to the established trails, which leave the John Muir Trail every few miles and ascend gentle valleys toward the lakes nestled under serrated peaks. Yet this region proves eminently suited to the traveler who prefers cross-country travel. For example, the pleasant, trailless High Route traverse from Superior Lake to Thousand Island Lake offers easy walking with only a few rough sections. Elevation differences on this eight-mile jaunt never exceed 900 feet at any one place, a relief to those hikers weary of more extreme ups and downs.

High Route trekkers interested in geology will especially appreciate the initial part of this segment, for the Ritter Range provides colorful and convoluted topography. François Matthes, the famed geologist of the Sierra Nevada, once noted the geological significance of the region: "When you climb Mount Ritter, you climb the core of one of the ancestral mountains that were formed more than a hundred million years before the present Sierra Nevada was uplifted." Josiah Whitney, leader of the California Geological Survey in the 1860s, stated that the rock of the Ritter Range was granitic, but the learned scientist was in error. The mottled, dark gray rock is actually ancient lava that has been metamorphosed beyond all recognition.

At Glacier Lake Pass, the watershed boundary between the San Joaquin River's Middle and North forks, the traveler stands on the threshold of a region so rarely visited that for the following few days it is easy to imagine being the first to explore the slabs and meadowlands. And, indeed, there is a scarcity of information about the original explorations around the headwaters of the North Fork. Theodore Solomons, whose peregrinations farther south are documented elsewhere in this book, wandered through this wild region in 1897, when for the third time he stood atop Mount Ritter. Since this ascent was made from the headwaters of the Merced River, Solomons must have crossed the North Fork of the San Joaquin; alas, his exact itinerary is not known.

Blue Lake Pass, the High Route saddle just south of Foerster Peak, first was crossed in 1907; a group of fifteen adventurers from that year's Sierra Club outing made the journey from the headwaters of the Merced River to Thousand Island Lake. Other Sierra Club parties traversed the identical route in subsequent years. Later, Walter Starr, Jr., briefly described the cross-country trek in his well-known trail guide, concluding his somewhat vague account with a succinct and accurate statement: "This is a fairly rough but short and spectacular route for knapsackers. . . ."

Straightforward cross-country travel between Blue Lake Pass and Tuolumne Meadows proves impossible because of Mount Lyell and its radiating western ridges, most of which harbor steep north sides unpleasant and even dangerous to the backpacker. Thus, the final few days of this segment of the High Route involve hiking along infrequently traveled trails in the backcountry of Yosemite National Park. As one approaches the commercial camp near Vogelsang Lake—some eight miles south of Tuolumne Meadows—hordes of hikers appear once again, a sure indication that a road lies nearby.

Approaches

Devil's Postpile National Monument, the southern terminus of this segment of the High Route, lies near the end of a road that leaves U.S. Highway 395 and crosses the Sierra crest just north of that downhill skier's paradise, Mammoth Mountain. Visitors must park at the ski area and take a shuttle bus over the crest and down to Devil's Postpile. This efficient system, inaugurated in the summer of 1979 by the U.S. Forest Service, greatly relieves the traffic congestion along the narrow road that parallels the Middle Fork of the San Joaquin River. At Red's Meadow, a mile from Devil's Postpile, are a store and a ranger station; several campgrounds are located in the vicinity.

The northern terminus of this section of the High Route is Tuolumne Meadows, a well-known attraction on the trans-Sierra road that crosses Tioga Pass. This strikingly beautiful region offers the visitor a store, gas station, and ranger station, as well as an enormous campground.

An appealing loop trip can alleviate transportation problems for those hikers who leave their cars at Mammoth Mountain. Leave the High Route at the Vogelsang High Sierra Camp and follow the trail that heads east to meet the John Muir Trail in Lyell Canyon. From this junction twenty miles of relatively easy walking leads to the shuttle-bus stop at Agnew Meadows.

The High Route

Devil's Postpile to Minaret Lake

The famed geological wonder known as Devil's Postpile is worth examining in some detail, for it is one of the finest North American examples of columnar basalt. Many of its sixty-foot columns rise straight as an arrow; others curve sensuously. Those who take the time to visit the top of the formation will be pleasantly surprised, for glaciers have burnished the severed tops of the columns, forming a charming mosaic.

Curious trekkers may wonder about the origin of the formation. Several hundred thousand years ago, a gigantic flow of black basaltic lava spewed forth from a fissure near present-day Mammoth Pass. After covering the canyon floor to a depth of about 500 feet, the cooling basalt contracted into columns. Most of these columns had either five or six sides, but a few were formed with three, four, seven, or eight sides. Tens of thousands of years later, the so-called Middle Fork Glacier steadily carried away most of the region's basalt, leaving only scattered, unyielding outcrops—like the Postpile—for modern visitors to appreciate.

Sheepherders were responsible for naming this geological curiosity. According to an 1894 report by Theodore Solomons, "in every scenic freak the sheepherder recognizes the handiwork of his Satanic majesty. This forma-

tion is therefore known to local fame as the Devil's Wood-
pile." By 1911, when the national monument was established, the name had evolved into its present form.

The High Route—here following the John Muir Trail
—crosses the Middle Fork on a sturdy bridge just a few
hundred yards north of Devil's Postpile. Ascending gently
upward, the trail skirts minor basaltic remnants. The
ubiquitous pumice of the Mammoth Mountain region
blankets the ground, making the hiking less than pleasant.
About one-and-a-half miles from the bridge the traveler
meets the Beck Lakes Trail coming in from the west. Bid
temporary farewell to the John Muir Trail; the High
Route will follow it for only one more mile, many days
hence.

Ascend the Beck Lakes Trail as it switchbacks up a
hillside covered with splendid examples of western white
pine, mountain hemlock, and red fir. Five miles west of the
river the trail drops a few hundred feet into the King
Creek drainage. Not far beyond lies Superior Lake, a narrow body of water in a pleasant, forested setting. During
the seven or so miles from Devil's Postpile, the traveler
has gained slightly more than 2,000 vertical feet. Free at
last from the huge canyon of the Middle Fork, the hiker
stands again at the gateway to timberline country.

From the west end of Superior Lake continue along the
trail, by now only a faint path. Within a few hundred feet
the traveler enters the finest stand of mountain hemlocks
on the entire High Route. Small purple cones, cylindrical

in shape, grow in profusion throughout the upper half of the tree; in late season thousands of fallen cones, as delicate as the conifer itself, blanket the ground. It is easy to see why John Muir called the hemlock "the very loveliest tree in the forest."

Leaving this idyllic place about a quarter of a mile beyond Superior Lake, the High Route begins ascending an easy 600-foot slope that ends at 10,200-foot Nancy Pass, the conspicuous gap west of Peak 10,532. The view from the pass is by far the finest seen from the High Route since Mammoth Crest. Red Slate Mountain, displaying a distinctive snow couloir, rises prominently to the south; less identifiable is the Mount Abbot group, but to its right is the sharp outline of that familiar High Route peak, Seven Gables. The panorama to the north proves far more interesting, for the peaks are intimate and colorful. The southern spires of the Minarets loom close at hand, and Mount Ritter and Banner Peak dominate the background. A minuscule portion of Minaret Lake—the next major High Route landmark—is visible below massive Volcanic Ridge. The route toward the lake should be studied carefully from Nancy Pass, for it is a bit tricky. Avoid descending to the meadowlands directly below; instead, the object is to diagonal down and to the left, losing as little elevation as possible.

Descend a few hundred feet of unstable talus below Nancy Pass, then wander left toward the uppermost visible trees. From here drop down a precipitous slope to easier ground, then contour to the north. Pass over the inconspicuous saddle west of Peak 9,833 and descend into the lush meadowlands below Deadhorse Lake. An imposing, dark horn of rock interrupts the skyline to the north: this is the first of the Minarets, Riegelhuth Minaret. Contour north under this striking formation to the southeast shore of Minaret Lake.

For more than half a century this beautifully situated lake has been a favorite base camp for mountaineering activities, and it is easy to see why. Triangular Clyde Minaret dominates the skyline above the far side of the lake. First climbed in 1928 by the legendary Norman Clyde, the 12,281-foot dagger offers the competent rock-climber half a dozen routes, including one so excellent it was included in the book *Fifty Classic Climbs of North America,* by the author and Allen Steck. This demanding ascent, first accomplished in 1963, lies near the center of the face as viewed from the lake.

From the same side of the lake the hiker can spy Michael Minaret, the second-highest pinnacle of the Minarets, peeking out from behind the left-hand skyline of the highest peak, Clyde Minaret. This remote, needlelike pinnacle, invisible from most viewpoints, occupies a sacred niche in the range's mountaineering history. It was here, close to the peak's summit, that Walter Starr, Jr., fell to his death while solo climbing in August 1933. His body, discovered by Norman Clyde, was entombed on the ledge where it was found.

Other climbers have been killed or injured while seeking these airy summits, and inexperienced persons
tempted to scale the heights should heed these words of
Charles Michael, a famous solo climber of the 1920s:
"There is no friendliness about the Minarets. When seen
from a distance they wear a black and sinister look. Precipitous walls rise to the sky-line, where beetling crags cut
raggedly against the horizon. There are no gentle slopes
to beckon one to the summit; rather does the scowling
sheerness warn one off. The spirit of the mountain is the
spirit of defiance. . . ."

Minaret Lake to Whitebark Pass

After absorbing the sterling view, the High Route hiker
must reach the western shore of Minaret Lake. After midseason this is done most easily by traversing the south
shore; in early season a massive snowbank drops directly
into the lake and bars easy progress, especially in the
morning, when the snow can be rock hard. It takes only
twenty minutes longer to wind around the lake on its
north side; at the outlet the traveler passes the western
terminus of the Minaret Lake Trail, which leads four miles
east to join the John Muir Trail.

From the west side of Minaret Lake ascend a rough
path up the north side of the creek that is seen above. Aim
for the right side of the broad saddle forming the "dam"
of Cecile Lake, the next higher body of water. Leave the
creek when it veers toward Clyde Minaret and ascend

talus and scree to a short class 2–3 slot that slices through a steep cliff band; the lake lies only a few feet beyond.

Traverse easy talus around the north shore of austere Cecile Lake to its outlet, a marvelous juxtaposition of water and metamorphic rock. From here the hiker has an excellent view of the main Minaret Ridge. Clyde Minaret appears more ridgelike than needlelike now; it was on the steep wall above its pocket-sized glacier that Norman Clyde made his solo first ascent. To the north is a classic view of Mount Ritter and its satellite, Banner Peak; this is the final time the traveler can take in the "traditional" view visible for so long on the High Route. Directly below Cecile Lake lies Iceberg Lake, a body of water so sheltered from the summer's sun that it remains free of ice only three or four months a year.

From the outlet of Cecile Lake follow a well-defined path down a steep, unpleasant slope high above the eastern shore of Iceberg Lake. The descent usually involves crossing a major snowfield, but by midseason hikers have created a distinct trench in the snow, making the passage quite safe. The hiker eventually meets the lake at its outlet, a singularly peaceful place.

From the northern shoreline of Iceberg Lake, follow a good path north toward Ediza Lake. After about 300 yards leave the trail, veer left, and drop down minor cliffs and grassy slopes until it is possible to cross the tumultuous creek draining Iceberg Lake. Continue along—aiming toward Banner Peak—for a few hundred yards to a fine viewpoint; the next few miles of the High Route lie in full view. The immediate object is to reach a prominent cascade on the stream that flows into Ediza Lake from the Mount Ritter massif.

Cross the creek just below the cascade and follow a faint path upstream. Leaving isolated stands of conifers behind, continue upstream, aiming directly toward the saddle separating the awesome twin peaks above. Upon reaching a bleak tarn at the 10,000-foot level, the High Route abruptly changes direction, ascending a gentle incline northeast toward the Nydiver Lakes. As soon as the first of these lakes is spotted, begin ascending diagonally over toward Whitebark Pass, the wide saddle immediately west of Peak 10,704. Just before reaching this pass, the traveler will come across a superb specimen of whitebark pine, its ancient trunk seemingly welded to the rock.

At Whitebark Pass the hiker stands astride the divide separating Shadow Creek from Garnet Lake, now visible below. A glance back to the south proves rewarding, for the serrated Minarets tower dramatically above the visible portions of Cecile and Iceberg lakes.

Whitebark Pass to Glacier Lake Pass

On the north side of Whitebark Pass a snowfield lingers until late season; do not attempt to descend it without an ice axe. Instead, move about fifty feet to the east, where a steep and loose defile drops 100 feet before debouching onto a talus slope. This, in turn, leads down to the slabs and meadowlands near the lake immediately above the head of Garnet Lake.

A gentle stroll to the north soon takes the High Route hiker to yet another watershed boundary, this one a 10,100-foot saddle overlooking the vast expanse of Thousand Island Lake. Whether or not 1,000 islands actually exist proves irrelevant, for the name eloquently conveys the idea. No other Sierra lake is so dotted with islands as this mile-and-a-half-long body of water. On a trip in 1892, Theodore Solomons became intrigued by the scenic wonder, calling it—and its environs—"an almost ideal Alpine landscape. One unconsciously looks along the shore of the lake for the ubiquitous Swiss Hotel."

Easy walking from the pass leads down to the extensive meadowlands that lie between the lake and several ponds just above it. In midseason these meadows display numerous varieties of wildflowers, with paintbrush predominating. Contrasting vividly with such luxuriance is the somber façade of Banner Peak, exactly 3,000 feet above.

Continue northwest across gentle terrain for nearly half a mile until reaching a major stream descending from the flanks of Mount Davis. Turn west up this brook—the chief inlet stream of Thousand Island Lake—and ascend terrain speckled with solitary groves of whitebark pine. Timberline country rarely offers more pleasant walking than it does in this region, for as the traveler strides alongside the marvelously clear and turbulent creek, the nearby peaks tower dramatically overhead and lakes glimmer in the distance.

The observant hiker undoubtedly will spot several pairs of dippers, or water ouzels, along this creek, for the habitat proves absolutely perfect for this curious bird. Never more than a few inches from water—and often either partially or completely submerged—these stocky, gray denizens of Sierra waters intrigued John Muir, who once wrote a 5,000-word essay lauding them. In almost every Sierra stream, he wrote, "you will surely find its complementary Ouzel, flitting about in the spray, diving in foaming eddies, whirling like a leaf among beaten foam-bells; ever vigorous and enthusiastic, yet self-contained, and neither seeking nor shunning your company." Commenting on their cheerful disposition even in a storm, when other birds cower in abject misery, Muir found that the dippers "could no more help exhaling sweet song than a rose sweet fragrance." The neophyte birdwatcher should have no trouble identifying the dipper: its chunky form constantly bobs up and down, and, in flight, the bird flies just above the surface of the water, following each and every bend in the stream.

The High Route traveler next proceeds southwest up a shallow basin toward the low saddle separating Banner Peak from Mount Davis. Until late season a massive snowfield guards the final approach to the pass; but this obstacle is not particularly steep, and the hiker should reach 11,158-foot Glacier Lake Pass with little trouble. From this desolate spot there is a unique view of the sensuously shaped glacier on Mount Ritter's north side. Originating at the Banner-Ritter col, this narrow glacier ends just above Lake Catherine, a rockbound lake in an austere setting devoid of vegetation.

Glacier Lake Pass to the Twin Island Lakes

Drop down a few feet from Glacier Lake Pass to the shoreline of Lake Catherine and follow stable talus around the lake's north side to the flat benches at its western end. Continue west a few hundred feet to a skein of tarns, then follow these southwest. Just beyond the outlet of the final tarn, the hiker arrives abruptly at a dropoff overlooking the chasm of the North Fork of the San Joaquin River. Across this awesome gorge—and only a mile and a quarter as the raven flies—the traveler can spot one of the Twin Island Lakes; the High Route soon will traverse the shores of both these remote lakes.

Below the viewpoint, a wild stream roars headlong down slabs and cliffs. In this area the backpacker must wander carefully down the class 2 ramps and ledges bordering the stream. After a few hundred yards of this fascinating terrain, the hiker reaches the brink of an eighty-foot waterfall that plunges into the tarn shown on the map at the 10,650-foot level. Since this cliff is impassable, traverse instead across ledges on the small, domelike outcrop to the north. The following stage of the descent involves short class 3 cliffs that separate complex ledge systems. Hikers should consider having the most experienced person in the group reconnoiter the next few hundred feet while the others wait for the verdict. Since the exposure in this area is minimal, little danger is involved; nevertheless, this section could result in a few anxious moments for the beginning backpacker.

Not far below this rugged section, the traveler reaches a conspicuous meadow situated several hundred feet north of the main stream. This isolated glade, perched above an alarmingly steep cliff, offers the hiker a temporary respite from the world of stone. The easiest way to circumvent the 500-foot cliff below is to leave the meadow and contour north a few hundred yards until it is possible to work down a prominent section of rust-colored rock. Soon the hiker will intersect a major creek, the one shown on the map as originating near the summit of Mount Davis. Follow this frantically rushing stream down to the junction with the original creek; nearby is a welcome grove of lodgepole pines, the largest conifers seen along the route since the environs of Ediza Lake.

From this isolated grove of pines at 9,900 feet, a rough path leads north 100 yards along a bench before dropping down into a loose gully. This proves to be an excellent place from which to study the route over to the Twin Island Lakes. The High Route does not descend very far into the classic, U-shaped valley of the North Fork, but rather contours around its head. Although this section is not at all difficult, it is somewhat complicated, involving numerous minor elevation changes as well as tricky routefinding through labyrinthine granite corridors.

The object is to reach the south end of the northern

Twin Island Lake, and once this goal is attained, the High Route wanderer faces a dilemma not often encountered in the High Sierra: a significant river crossing. Because of the complex topography near the outlet of the lake, there is only one way to cross the infant North Fork, and that is to wade. The sound of the raging river just below the outlet reminds the traveler not to falter in midstream, but the crossing proves easier than it looks; the current is sluggish, and the water is only three feet deep. The most experienced—or the bravest—person in the group should take charge and ferry the others' packs across the twenty-foot-wide obstruction.

With this minor hindrance behind, the backpacker ascends a gentle slope that levels out near the north end of the southern Twin Island Lake. Turn this infrequently visited body of water on the left by means of monolithic granite slabs. In the south end of the lake reposes an island so aesthetically pleasing that it would be totally appropriate in the garden of a Japanese temple.

Twin Island Lakes to Blue Lake Pass

During the next few miles, the High Route traveler traverses one of the most untrammeled sections of the entire 195-mile trek. There are no ducks, no fireplace scars, no bits of trash, and few footprints. It must remain this way.

From the south end of the southern Twin Island Lake, follow a gentle valley 200 yards south to a grass-covered pass offering an extensive view into the glacier-carved valley of the North Fork. Climb the incline west of this pass for a few hundred feet, then traverse around the long ridge radiating south from Peak 11,596. Ascend diagonally into the valley west of this ridge until reaching a wild and beautiful lake at 10,200 feet. Continue west across a pleasant basin distinguished by its easy walking.

From a grassy gap north of Peak 10,280 ascend a gentle hillside west until level with the top of the peaklet, then contour straight across medium-sized talus until reaching a dark bluff. A fabulous view unfolds at this spot. Below, winding west in graceful curves, lies Bench Canyon, surely one of the most sublime valleys in the range. Minuscule groves of conifers harmonize perfectly with shining slabs and glistening brooks. The view back to the east is equally stunning, for the northern half of the Ritter Range fills the sky. On the escarpment beneath Glacier Lake Pass, the hiker will spy a thin ribbon of white—the endless cascade beside which the hiker recently zigzagged. To the right of lofty Mount Ritter lies spectacular Peak 12,344; its jagged crest was not reached until 1964, making it the last major Sierra summit to be climbed.

An easy descent from the dark bluff leads down into Bench Canyon, and the route for the next mile is both obvious and easy. At the 10,100-foot level—near the stream junction shown on the map—a fairyland setting is encountered. Isolated clumps of whitebark and lodgepole pines rise alongside massive granite boulders, and on the hillside to the north is a twenty-acre meadow that in midseason is blanketed by more wildflowers than the mind can comprehend. Lupine predominates, but there are dozens of other species, including paintbrush, elephant head, pennyroyal, and penstemon. Amid such splendor, it is nearly impossible to avoid cavorting like a child.

At some point the traveler must move on again, forsaking this fertile wonderland for the subalpine zone above. Ascend slabs alongside the south branch of the main creek until coming upon a lake with a prosaic but accurate name: Blue Lake. From here the hiker is afforded an excellent view of the next obstacle on the High Route, the 700-foot climb up to Blue Lake Pass. This saddle—on the eastern boundary of Yosemite National Park—lies just to the left of Foerster Peak, which can be identified by its serrated left-hand skyline. Another way to recognize the correct pass is to find the first saddle to the right of a small, brown, U-shaped notch. The ascent to the pass proves amazingly easy, involving grassy slopes, low-angled slabs, and short stretches of stable talus.

From the 11,200-foot pass—the highest High Route elevation reached since Mammoth Crest—the hiker can pause and absorb the extensive view. The entire Ritter Range, jagged and forbidding, lies visible. Michael Minaret, the final resting place of Walter Starr, Jr., proves remarkably spirelike from this angle. Farther to the south rises an array of the central Sierra's highest summits, including Mounts Abbot, Humphreys, and Goddard. Still farther south, barely visible through the haze, is the isolated Kaweah Peaks Ridge, slightly more than ninety miles distant.

On the west side of the pass there is an unparalleled panorama of the Clark Range, just seven miles away. Its four major summits are, from left to right, Merced Peak, Red Peak, Gray Peak, and Mount Clark itself. This latter peak, once known as the Obelisk, first was climbed by that fascinating pioneer, Clarence King. Although King's exploits on Mount Whitney remain far better known than those on Mount Clark, the latter peak was more difficult technically, and King returned to his camp "well pleased that the Obelisk had not vanquished us."

Northwest of the Clark Range, and just right of the summit of nearby Peak 11,210, lies Mount Hoffmann, the first major Sierra summit to be climbed and still one of the most popular today. Hidden from the viewer, the Tioga Pass Highway traverses the timberline country just south of this peak.

Foerster Peak, the 12,058-foot summit just north of Blue Lake Pass, was named in honor of Lewis Foerster, a young cavalryman. In 1895 he was a member of a detachment sent by the federal government to evict the cattlemen and sheepherders who were illegally bringing stock into the fragile landscape of the newly created Yosemite National Park. Thirty-nine years after he had helped patrol this region, Foerster returned with a Sierra Club group and climbed the peak his commanding officer, Lieutenant Nathaniel McClure, had named for him.

Blue Lake Pass to Vogelsang Pass

After taking in the view, drop down steep but fairly

stable talus on the west side of Blue Lake Pass; a few short cliffs intervene occasionally, but they are bypassed easily. After a descent of approximately 400 feet, the hiker arrives on the shores of a rockbound lake. From its outlet, begin a marvelous downhill traverse across subalpine meadowlands occasionally interrupted by streams so clear that the stones on their bottoms glimmer like jewels. Stroll northwest through this idyllic landscape toward the prominent, grass-covered benches lying underneath Peak 11,-210. Upon reaching these, turn left and drop down forested bluffs. The Isberg Pass Trail, met in the wide saddle east of Peak 9,958, might be overlooked if the traveler is not watchful, for it is rather inconspicuous in this area. If the members of the party spread out when approaching the saddle, there will be less chance of striding across it unknowingly.

Follow the path north through the dense forest to the dropoff overlooking the vast canyon of the Lyell Fork of the Merced River. During the 1,000-foot descent through stands of lodgepole pines and mountain hemlocks, the hiker gains an excellent view of the park's highest summit, 13,114-foot Mount Lyell. To its left lies the barren, uninteresting basin at the headwaters of Hutching Creek; it is easy to see why the High Route temporarily eschews the subalpine zone in favor of more benign country to the west.

The trail descends the precipitous southern flank of the Lyell Fork Canyon by means of a prominent break in the cliffs, a feature appreciated by Walter Starr, Allen Chickering, and Theodore Solomons in July 1896. These three pioneers had just embarked on a journey that would prove to be the first complete pack trip ever made between Yosemite and Kings Canyon. Starr called this particular stretch of their route—then trailless, of course—a "perfect ledge . . . made-to-order. . . ."

The Lyell Fork can be crossed on any one of several fallen-log bridges. Continue along the trail as it ascends in a gentle manner along another "made-to-order" ledge. Sierra junipers, easily recognized by their massive trunks, line the trail in this section; this is the first High Route appearance of this species since LeConte Canyon. In his *Mountains of California,* John Muir described this tree in a rather unkind fashion: "Its fine color and odd picturesqueness always catch an artist's eye, but to me the Juniper seems a singularly dull and taciturn tree, never speaking to one's heart."

About four miles from the Lyell Fork crossing, the little-used path arrives at the brink of the granite-walled gorge of Lewis Creek. Just as the trail begins its abrupt descent into this watershed, the traveler catches a glimpse of one of the world's greatest geological wonders, Half Dome; only the upper reaches of this famous formation are visible.

North of the viewer rises another geological oddity, Matthes Crest. Named after noted geologist François Matthes, the airy summit of this serrated white blade of granite long has been the goal of rockclimbers.

After meeting a major trail at Lewis Creek, turn right

and ascend through the forest. The next few miles prove exceptionally charming, especially to hikers who have spent the past few days traversing austere timberline country. Lewis Creek—more of a river than a creek—churns frantically down monolithic slabs of granite. The side streams are vigorous also, especially Florence Creek, which provides the hiker with the most awesome display of cascading water on the entire High Route.

After passing the turnoff to Bernice Lake, the trail ascends through timberline country for about 800 vertical feet to Vogelsang Pass, a grassy saddle containing—until late season—an attractive tarn. The panorama east toward the subalpine basin above Gallison Lake reveals the upper portions of the Mount Lyell group.

Vogelsang Pass to Tuolumne Meadows

The descent from Vogelsang Pass proves trivial, and the hiker soon reaches the shores of Vogelsang Lake. From its outlet, a pleasant locale for a rest stop, the traveler enjoys an all-encompassing view. To the west, some eleven miles distant, rises Half Dome; its profile here is a mirror image of the one that multitudes see from the floor of Yosemite Valley. To the northwest, across Fletcher Creek, enormous slabs of exfoliating granite cover acres of landscape; it is easy to understand why this geological curiosity, common in granitic country, often is compared to the layer-by-layer peeling of an onion.

To the right of the peeling granite slabs lie the incongruous cabins of the commercial establishment known as the Vogelsang High Sierra Camp; the American flag waving above the main building seems oddly out of place in this wilderness setting. Above the flag, far in the distance, rises the white bulk of the northern Sierra's most prominent landmark, Mount Conness. Its imposing southwest face, visible from Vogelsang Lake, was the first big wall ever climbed in the High Sierra. Warren Harding, fresh from his victory on Yosemite Valley's El Capitan, led this four-day ascent in 1959.

The High Route drops down to the commercial camp, then ascends gently north to broad Tuolumne Pass, the watershed boundary between the Merced and Tuolumne rivers. From this saddle an agreeable walk, marred only slightly by the increasingly frequent signs of civilization, leads down the forested slopes alongside Rafferty Creek for about five miles. Upon intersecting the John Muir Trail, turn left and proceed west for nearly three-quarters of a mile to another signed junction. Leave the John Muir Trail—for good—and follow the trail north. After a scant hundred yards, this new trail crosses the Lyell Fork of the Tuolumne River at a strikingly beautiful location. The placid water, hitting a barrier of granite, pours through an amazing channel before coursing into the deep green pools below. It is a magical place indeed.

Five hundred yards farther north, the trail crosses the Dana Fork of the Tuolumne; turn right immediately after crossing the bridge and stroll a few hundred feet to the Tuolumne Meadows High Sierra Camp, the northern terminus of this section of the High Route.

Reversing the Route

Since the entire northern portion of this segment of the High Route follows well-marked trails, there should be no routefinding problems when heading south until the hiker is ready to leave the Isberg Pass Trail and begin the cross-country trek toward the Ritter Range. Not long after attaining the valley rim south of the Lyell Fork of the Merced River, the little-used path descends a small bluff and enters a level, forested section. Leave the trail about 300 yards south of the bluff and head due east through the dense forest. After surmounting a short but steep slope, the hiker reaches the grassy benches underneath Peak 11,210. From these, head southeast across meadowlands toward Blue Lake Pass, the conspicuous gap immediately to the right of Foerster Peak. The route across the pass is obvious.

Farther along, it is important to leave Bench Canyon at the correct place; otherwise, numerous cliff bands will be encountered. Quit the main creek at the stream junction shown on the map at 9,700 feet and work diagonally uphill to the east. When above all the cliff bands—at approximately 10,200 feet—begin the long traverse into the basin to the east. The next section, leading to the Twin Island Lakes, loses a few hundred feet of elevation as it circles the ridge dropping from Peak 11,596.

From the outlet of the southern Twin Island Lake, the traveler can pause to study the intimidating headwall leading up to Glacier Lake Pass, the wide gap left of Banner Peak. After leaving the northern lake and contouring around the head of the valley, ascend a steep slope lying 100 yards left of a spectacular cascade. Next, traverse right on a bench over to the creek, meeting it in a solitary grove of lodgepole pines. Ascend the left branch of the creek to an area of reddish rock high above, then work up and slightly right over complex terrain to Glacier Lake Pass.

There should be little difficulty accomplishing the next few miles over to Cecile Lake, but from its southern shore the hiker may be delayed briefly while searching for the top of the class 2–3 slot leading down toward Minaret Lake. The key to finding this narrow passage is to proceed to the very lowest point of the lake's "dam," only twenty or thirty feet above water level. A short scouting trip from here quickly reveals the top of the slot and the rudimentary path below it.

Locating Nancy Pass when traveling south provides the most significant routefinding exercise of this segment of the route. From the bluffs just south of Minaret Lake the hiker can identify Nancy Pass as the first saddle to the left of the large, black, multisummited peak that rises a mile to the south. Another method of verifying the correct pass is that it lies near the junction of the black rock with the red-colored rock that continues east. Once the correct gap has been located, there should be no problem reaching it if one remembers to keep to the right en route, circling the head of the valley.

Alternate Routes

It is possible to bypass certain sections of the first part
of this High Route segment by using parts of the John
Muir Trail in conjunction with the spur trails radiating
west from it in this region. A study of the map reveals
these obvious routes.

The Ritter Range can be crossed in several places south
of Glacier Lake Pass, but because of the enormous elevation drops from these passes into the canyon of the North
Fork of the San Joaquin River, such alternate routes are
feasible only for strong and exploration-minded backpackers.

To avoid the traverse—and river crossing—from the
Twin Island Lakes to Bench Canyon, follow the unmain-
tained trail down the North Fork to its junction with
Bench Canyon and then head west up the canyon. This
variation, though not much longer than the High Route,
requires an elevation loss—and subsequent gain—of more
than 1,000 feet.

In the late season, experienced talus walkers can cross
the high ridge connecting Foerster and Electra peaks, thus
bypassing Blue Lake Pass. This route lingers longer in the
alpine zone than does the High Route and, as an added
attraction, passes through one of the loveliest glades in the
High Sierra, Lyell Fork Meadow. Nevertheless, this alternate proves far more demanding than the High Route and
should be considered only by adventurous backpackers

who wish to avoid trails at any cost. Leave the High Route
at the dark bluff met just prior to the descent into Bench
Canyon and diagonal north up into the basin lying between Peaks 11,156 and 11,537. Ascend loose talus northwest to the basin's highest lake; Mount Ansel Adams, a
prominent tower not indicated by name on the map, rises
just above this lake. The 11,600-foot notches on either side
of this striking peak are now easily accessible; from either
one a steep, loose gully drops toward the Lyell Fork of the
Merced River. These gullies are safe only when they are
free of snow. After reaching the river, pass west through
Lyell Fork Meadow and rejoin the High Route downstream.

Mountaineering en Route

Pridham Minaret

As mentioned earlier, Minaret Lake provides an excellent base camp for mountaineers. Because of the exceedingly rugged nature of the area, though, there are few
peaks that can be climbed by backpackers untrained in
the use of the rope and ice axe. There are exceptions, however. To the south of the lake lies Pridham Minaret, the
second peaklet from the east on the ridge south of the
lake. A scramble up snowfields, gullies, and talus
takes the climber to the saddle separating Pridham
and Riegelhuth, the easternmost pinnacle. From here a

talus slope leads to the 11,000-foot summit, a fine viewpoint.

Volcanic Ridge

An even more spectacular view awaits the hiker who reaches the top of Volcanic Ridge, the 11,501-foot mass just north of Minaret Lake. The summit is a popular goal because of this panorama, even though the climb itself is not especially interesting. The usual route begins from the north shore of the lake and ascends a long, grassy slope about 1,100 feet to a saddle. From here turn left and scramble up talus to the summit ridge. Isolated from the main Minaret chain, the peak offers a bird's-eye view perhaps unmatched on the High Route. The traveler can return via a different route to make a loop trip: from the summit, drop northeast down talus until it becomes feasible to descend a steep slope that levels off in the valley containing the Minaret Mine. Last worked in 1930, the site contains several weathered buildings and numerous tailings attractive to the rockhound. From the isolated mine, head down the creek for about three-quarters of a mile until it becomes possible to ascend a short slope on the west. From its top, follow easy terrain back to Minaret Lake.

Mount Ritter

Mount Ritter has been a popular goal of mountaineers for more than a century. Clarence King, that early explorer of the High Sierra—and later the first director of the United States Geological Survey—attempted the enormous peak in 1866 but failed some 500 feet below the top, calling the remaining section "inaccessible." After a thrilling climb, John Muir reached the lofty summit in October 1872. Since then thousands of mountaineers have stood upon the 13,157-foot summit, admiring a panorama that encompasses most of the northern High Sierra.

There are several routes up Mount Ritter's flanks; two of these are feasible for High Route hikers. Muir's descent route—the Southeast Glacier Route—is reached easily from the High Route. Although some glacier travel is encountered, an ice axe rarely is needed, and the ascent is practical for strong backpackers competent on class 3 terrain. Leave the High Route at the bleak tarn at the head of the stream above Ediza Lake and scramble up snow gullies and easy slabs to the glacier, which is mostly hidden from below. Ascend the glacier until it is possible to transfer onto the rocks bordering its northern edge. From here talus slopes—sometimes buried by snow—can be followed easily for the remaining 1,000 feet to the summit.

The second route on Mount Ritter is interesting historically, for it was that peripatetic explorer Theodore Solomons who made the first ascent. Climbing alone in 1892, the twenty-two-year-old carried an 8 × 10 view camera on the ascent, returning to civilization with the first high-quality photographs ever made in the alpine regions of the High Sierra. His West Side Route, easier but less interesting than the Southeast Glacier Route, branches from the High Route near Lake Catherine. From the top of the great dropoff overlooking the canyon of the North Fork of the San Joaquin River, work south along a chain of rockbound lakes. From a point near the last lake—called by Solomons "a beautiful sheet of clear water"—ascend a steep and loose slope, interrupted on occasion by outcrops and gullies, for 2,000 feet to the summit.

Banner Peak

Banner Peak, Mount Ritter's satellite, is also a popular ascent, offering a panorama nearly equal to that of its loftier neighbor. Nearly all climbers ascend the final 1,000-foot slope from the saddle separating the two peaks, but unless the traveler has an ice axe—and knows how to use it—the steep eastern approach to this saddle is not recommended. The far easier northwestern approach leaves the High Route at Lake Catherine and ascends a moderately angled glacier—free of crevasses—all the way to the saddle. Steep talus then leads to the 12,945-foot summit.

Mount Davis

Hikers wary of snowfields and class 2–3 rock will discover that Mount Davis provides an interesting, if less challenging, alternative to Ritter and Banner. Leave the High Route at the west end of Lake Catherine and ascend a long, easy slope north to the summit plateau. There is an excellent view of the Mount Lyell group from the 12,311-foot summit.

Peak 9,988

Surely the easiest climb in proximity to the High Route is Peak 9,988, a rounded bump just south of the Twin Island Lakes. Although the fifteen-minute scramble from the shores of the southern Twin Island Lake hardly qualifies as a bona fide mountaineering exploit, the view of the Ritter Range and the stupendous canyon of the North Fork make this minor detour from the High Route a memorable one. The traveler who stands atop this peak at sundown surely will marvel at the alpenglow, which for a few minutes illuminates every peak of the Ritter Range.

Foerster Peak

Located just north of Blue Lake Pass, Foerster Peak is a class 2–3 scramble from the saddle. Norman Clyde made the first ascent in 1914 during one of his earliest forays into the range.

Vogelsang Peak

Another easy climb in proximity to the High Route is Vogelsang Peak. The traveler can begin climbing this mountain either from Vogelsang Pass or Vogelsang Lake; both routes are class 2. From the 11,516-foot summit there is a marvelous view of the sharp peaks surrounding Tuolumne Meadows.

6

Canyon Country:

Stanton Peak dominates the foreground in this view from Matter-horn Peak; Mount Conness rises in the right background.

Tuolumne Meadows
to Twin Lakes

I NUDGED MYSELF closer into the ledge and closed my eyes and thought "Oh what a life this is, why do we have to be born in the first place, and only so we can have our poor gentle flesh laid out to such impossible horrors as huge mountains and rock and empty space," and with horror I remembered the famous Zen saying, "When you get to the top of a mountain, keep climbing." The saying made my hair stand on end; it had been such cute poetry sitting on Alvah's straw mats. Now it was enough to make my heart pound and my heart bleed for being born at all. "In fact when Japhy gets to the top of that crag he *will* keep climbing, the way the wind's blowing. Well this old philosopher is staying right here," and I closed my eyes.

Jack Kerouac, describing
his emotions near the summit
of Matterhorn Peak.
From *The Dharma Bums.*

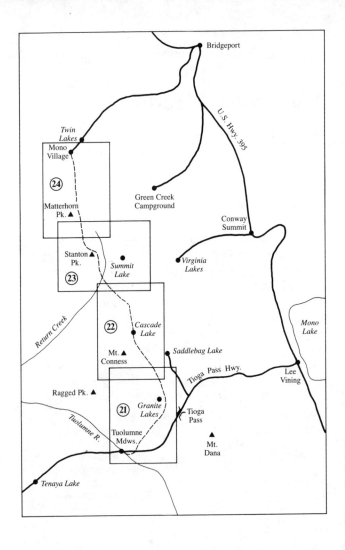

Bridgeport

U.S. Hwy. 395

Twin
Lakes
Mono
Village

(24)

Matterhorn
Pk. ▲

Green Creek
Campground

Conway
Summit

Stanton ▲
Pk.

(23)

Summit
Lake

Virginia
Lakes

Return Creek

(22)

Cascade
Lake

Mt. ▲
Conness

Saddlebag Lake

Mono
Lake

Tioga Pass Hwy.

Lee
Vining

Ragged Pk. ▲

Tuolumne R.

(21)

Granite
Lakes

Tioga
Pass

Tuolumne
Mdws.

▲
Mt.
Dana

Tenaya Lake

NORTH OF THE Tioga Pass Highway the High Route closely parallels the Sierra crest, never straying more than three miles from it and actually crossing it on three occasions. Except for the initial few miles and the final two miles, maintained trails are absent from this segment. Thus, for the majority of the trek, the traveler wanders cross-country through varied terrain, surmounting five major ridges along the way. In spite of such up-and-down travel, this segment is not particularly difficult; only one short section—below Stanton Pass—approaches class 3. Naturally, talus and snowfields are encountered occasionally, but since these obstacles are not unduly steep, they can be passed quickly by backpackers accustomed to class 2 terrain. Persons not fully acclimated to the heights also will appreciate this segment of the High Route, for only three times does the route penetrate the rarefied atmosphere above the 11,000-foot level.

The scenery along the route is outstanding from the very beginning: the vista south from the Gaylor Lakes includes virtually all the significant peaks in the southern half of Yosemite National Park. Later, from Sky Pilot Col, there is a sterling view of some of northern Yosemite's most conspicuous summits. From this same pass, the panorama in the opposite direction proves equally impressive, for the viewer gazes down upon the wildly colorful metamorphic rock that makes up the eastern flank of this part of the High Sierra.

Near the end of the journey, the High Route traveler becomes intimately involved with two of the most dramatic canyons in the northern Sierra. Virginia Canyon, the first of these features to be encountered, is a remarkably straight glacial trench that drops one vertical mile during its fifteen-mile descent to the raging Tuolumne River. The High Route crosses Virginia Canyon near its head, a striking locale graced by meadows and meandering brooks.

A few miles farther along, the High Route crosses into Spiller Creek Canyon, another marvelous geographical feature. Although far shorter than Virginia Canyon, this narrow valley is even more beautiful, surrounded as it is by the enormous masses of Whorl Mountain and Virginia Peak. On August 24, 1894, this remote valley was explored by federal cavalry who were attempting to evict sheepherders from the newly established national park. Seeking a passable stock route into nearby Matterhorn Canyon, Lieutenant Nathaniel McClure and several troopers followed Spiller Creek all the way to its source at Horse Creek Pass. For a brief time the High Route exactly follows the track of these pioneers.

Horse Creek Pass occupies an interesting—albeit minor—place in American literature, for it was from near here that an exhausted Jack Kerouac watched poet Gary Snyder scramble up the final slopes of Matterhorn Peak, the rocky hulk west of the pass. As recounted in *The Dharma Bums* (in which Snyder is known as Japhy Ryder), Kerouac later greeted his victorious friend with these words: "Dammit that yodel of triumph of yours was the most beautiful thing I ever heard in my life. I wish I'd had a tape recorder to take it down." Ryder/Snyder disagrees: "Those things aren't made to be heard by the people below." "By God you're right," Kerouac exclaims, "all those sedentary bums sitting around on pillows hearing the cry of the triumphant mountain smasher, they don't deserve it."

From Horse Creek Pass the final section of the High Route drops 3,500 vertical feet down Horse Creek to Twin Lakes, the northern terminus of the route. During this precipitous descent down yet another stupendous Sierra canyon, the hiker plunges in a matter of hours from the subalpine zone—with its sweeping aprons of granite and patches of minuscule wildflowers—into a less pleasant environment consisting of cars, cabins, sagebrush, and rattlesnakes. This abrupt transformation, typical of all descents down the steep eastern flank of the Sierra, proves especially dramatic to hikers who have remained in timberline country for any length of time. The solitude of such lovely places as Virginia Canyon and Soldier Lake will be recalled wistfully by High Route wanderers who, tramping forlornly through Mono Village, know that their journey has ended suddenly and far too soon.

Approaches

This final segment of the High Route begins at Tuolumne Meadows, those verdant acres traversed by the Tioga Pass Highway. As mentioned earlier, a ranger station, store, gas station, and campground are found at this popular locale. The actual trailhead for this segment is encountered at the Tuolumne Meadows High Sierra Camp, a mile or so east of the store.

Hikers wishing to intersect the High Route partway along it can do so by driving to Saddlebag Lake, a reservoir located several miles north of Tioga Pass. After following a trail around the reservoir, join the High Route at Cascade Lake.

The northern terminus of the High Route lies at Mono Village, a commercial zone located at the west end of Upper Twin Lake. This roadhead is reached easily from U.S. Highway 395 by following a paved road thirteen miles from the town of Bridgeport.

An excellent loop trip is available to hikers who leave cars at Tuolumne Meadows. Follow the High Route until half a mile short of Horse Creek Pass. Leave Spiller Creek at this point and climb up to the prominent saddle south of Matterhorn Peak. From this 11,400-foot pass the traveler is able to descend, in short order, to the trail in upper Matterhorn Canyon. Follow this trail on its circuitous journey south to Glen Aulin, a spectacular meadow on the Tuolumne River. From here a scenic trail leads upriver to Tuolumne Meadows.

The hiker also can depart the High Route at two other locations to join the above-mentioned trail. Upon reaching Virginia Canyon, simply descend the valley via a path that intersects the main one in a few miles. The traveler also may descend Spiller Creek Canyon a few miles until meeting the main trail.

The High Route

Tuolumne Meadows to the Gaylor Lakes

Owing to the configuration of the Tioga Pass Highway and the Dana Fork of the Tuolumne River, this segment of the High Route departs civilization in a rather circuitous fashion. Leave the huge parking lot adjoining the western edge of the Tuolumne Meadows High Sierra Camp and stroll south past several tent cabins until meeting a path that shoots southwest. After 100 yards cross the Dana Fork on a massive bridge, then continue on the path upstream for another 100 yards until reaching a marked trail junction. Take the path leading toward the Gaylor Lakes; within a few minutes it is possible to see, across the stream, the recently departed High Sierra Camp.

Paralleling the creek, the little-used trail alternately surmounts short hills and traverses long, flat wooded sections. After approximately two miles the path abruptly swings left to arrive on the banks of the Dana Fork. Since the park service has not seen fit to build a bridge here, the hiker must wade the twenty-foot-wide brook. Several good fording places will be discovered just upstream; the water is only a foot or two deep as it courses down flat granite slabs.

The Tioga Pass Highway—lying immediately north of this stream crossing—is the sole road the High Route crosses during its 195-mile length. It may be appropriate here to remember the men and women who fought so long to save the High Sierra from the short-sighted exploiters who, in their quest for timber and minerals, would have built roads in every region. Nowhere else in the continental United States can a person walk such a tremendous distance and come across so few signs of civilization.

The continuation of the trail on the north side of the thirty-foot-wide band of macadam is not immediately obvious; it lies a few steps west of the road bridge that crosses the creek flowing down from the Gaylor Lakes. The hiker can discern a trail sign partially hidden in the woods north of the highway. (Those who wish to begin their trek here and save a few miles of walking can locate this subtle trail junction most easily by driving east exactly three miles from the highway bridge that spans the Tuolumne River near the store.)

Follow the path north for about 300 yards until it ends at a well-traveled dirt road. Turn right and follow this road a few hundred yards through open woodlands and meadows until it makes a major curve to the left. At this point, within sight of the creek dropping from the Gaylor Lakes, leave the road and locate an unmarked trail on the right. This path begins to climb gently through a forest of lodgepole pines. Within a mile, the traveler encounters several pocket-sized meadows inundated with corn lilies, a spectacular plant recognized by the enormous oval leaves surrounding its tall, flowering stem. This conspicuous wildflower, mistakenly called "skunk cabbage" by many hikers, prefers habitats that remain wet throughout the summer.

The rushing creek is never out of earshot during this early section, although it is rarely visible. When the roar fades to a whisper, the hiker will know that timberline lies just ahead. Soon the traveler emerges into the splendid meadowlands of the lower portion of the basin containing the three Gaylor Lakes and the two Granite Lakes. For the first time on this route segment, the High Route hiker obtains an excellent view to the south. Mount Lyell, displaying its ample glacier, dominates the horizon, but the "cockscomb" pinnacles of the closer Cathedral Range also loom prominently.

The path winds up extensive meadowlands covered with flowers and thousands of granite boulders. Shallow tarns and clumps of lodgepole pines dot the landscape; this is timberline country at its best. All too quickly the traveler comes upon Lake 10,046, the lowest of the Gaylor Lakes. The trail fades and disappears soon after crossing the outlet stream, and the hiker then embarks on a long, trailless section extending nearly all the way to the route's northern terminus. This absence of a trail proves inconsequential at first, for the traveler ascends the easiest possible cross-country terrain to the outlet of the lower Granite Lake. This narrow body of water, bordered by granite cliffs and patches of greenery, occupies the bottom of a wide cirque nestled beneath the Sierra crest.

From the outlet of the lake ascend the grassy hillside to the northeast, aiming for the low saddle located left of Gaylor Peak, the conspicuous, red-colored hump to the east. During the pleasant stroll toward this landmark, the hiker becomes aware of a significant geological change. Dark chunks of metamorphic rock begin to appear in the granite-dotted meadows, and by the time the traveler has reached the uppermost Gaylor Lake, reposing directly underneath the steep northern flank of Gaylor Peak, the transformation is complete: slate and other metamorphic rocks have totally replaced the granite. The transition region between the two types of rock, called the "contact zone," is often several hundred feet wide and thus indistinct. But where it crosses the Sierra crest north of the

Granite Lakes, the border between light and dark is sharply delineated. The High Route parallels this particular contact zone for the remainder of its journey, traversing granitic countryside most of the time, but straying into the more colorful slate occasionally.

Gaylor Lakes to Mine Shaft Pass

From the western shoreline of the highest Gaylor Lake ascend north up the slate-covered hillside, following shallow gullies or rounded ridges as the terrain dictates. Soon, on the ridgecrest above, the hiker can spot the ruins of what the map indicates is the "Great Sierra Mine." This name appears to be a cartographer's invention, for in its heyday the site was known to its owners as the Mount Dana Summit Mine. Considering its distance from Mount Dana, the mine was inappropriately named, and the miners shortened the appellation to Summit Mine. Established in 1878, when traces of silver were discovered nearby, this lode—one of several hundred in an area extending north to Lundy Canyon—was worked in the winter as well as the summer, a fact that explains the buildings' three-foot-thick walls. The winters must have been singularly fierce, especially the one of 1879–80, when a nearby measuring station received nearly 800 inches of snow, double its normal amount. One certainly can empathize with an unnamed miner who descended into the desert town of Bodie one winter to collect the other miners' pay, but who found himself unable to leave the hospitable saloons for several weeks. Perhaps he reasoned that his half-frozen compatriots couldn't spend their money anyway.

It is not known exactly when activity at Summit Mine ceased, but nearby ventures folded for various reasons in the 1880s. Few of the region's many mines ever turned a profit, and because of its exceedingly remote location, it seems reasonably certain that Summit Mine was not financially successful. Nevertheless, the miners left a legacy for present-day hikers, who often stumble across mine shafts, tailings, remnants of buildings, and rusting machinery.

The uppermost ruins of Summit Mine lie directly astride the Sierra crest, and from this spectacular location the traveler enjoys a fine vista to the south. Mount Dana, slightly more than three miles distant, looms darkly against the skyline. Closer at hand is the red horn of Gaylor Peak, dominating the highest Gaylor Lake. Farther south, the viewer can distinguish only the summit rocks of Yosemite National Park's highest point, Mount Lyell; most of the mountain remains hidden by a shoulder of Mammoth Peak. Lyell's satellite peaks, including the black cone of Mount Maclure, rise in full view. Also prominent is Vogelsang Peak, recognized by its sharp, pyramidal summit. To its right, some eighteen miles from the mine, the traveler can discern Mount Clark, the guardian of south-central Yosemite.

To the north of Summit Mine there is a rather unexciting panorama. About the only thing to look at is the next portion of the High Route. The short-term goal is to reach Mine Shaft Pass, the wide, grassy gap perhaps 100 feet higher than Summit Mine and nearly half a mile distant. This minor, but important, High Route landmark lies just left of a prominent red knoll.

Contour northwest from the mine—keeping well above a tarn—for most of the distance to the pass, then stroll up a short slope, passing an old, filled-in mine shaft, to the saddle. The view north from Mine Shaft Pass more than compensates for the poor northern vista from Summit Mine. Mount Conness, last seen from the High Route near Tuolumne Pass, can be recognized by the remarkably uniform cliffs that guard its southeastern flank. The sharp upper portion of North Peak protrudes from behind the east ridge of Mount Conness. Directly in line with this landmark, and two-and-a-half miles across a wide valley, the viewer can spot a cascading stream emanating from a basin nestled below Mount Conness's east ridge. The High Route traveler soon will be winding up the slabs alongside this ribbon of white water. Also visible from the pass is the southern half of man-enlarged Saddlebag Lake, a popular vacation spot of fishermen.

For the next five miles or so the High Route wanders through beautiful country on the eastern side of the Sierra crest, and Mine Shaft Pass provides a fine opportunity for the hiker to pause and assimilate the dramatic contrasts between the landscapes on either side of the crest. Perhaps it will be the coloration of the peaks that catches the viewer's eye. On much of the eastern side the rounded mountains are composed of reddish-hued slate. But the crest itself and the region west of it are made up of sparkling white granite. The contact zone between these two types of rock is visible here for several miles. The vegetation provides another contrast, for there is a relative scarcity of large trees on the eastern flank of the Sierra. Since the crest acts as a barrier to the prevailing storm track, most of the winter's precipitation falls on the western slope of the range. When looking at Tioga Crest, immediately east of Saddlebag Lake, the viewer is gazing upon a desert mountain.

Mine Shaft Pass to Cascade Lake

Drop down a few hundred feet from Mine Shaft Pass to a wide bench that offers the curious hiker another glimpse into the legendary mining era. About 1,000 feet below, and in line with the Tioga Pass Highway, the traveler can spot the two remaining structures of Bennettsville, the former headquarters of the Great Sierra Consolidated Silver Company. Although the owners of this concern spent nearly a third of a million dollars in their quest for bullion, it appears that none of the ore so laboriously extracted by the miners ever reached the smelter.

From this viewpoint, begin a long, diagonal descent toward the northwest. The rocky terrain in this section looks rugged but proves surprisingly gentle. Snowfields blanket some of this traverse until late season, but they are not steep; indeed, they can provide a pleasant alternative to the slate. Work down rocky shelves covered with windblown whitebark pines until reaching Spuller Lake, a lovely jewel whose salient feature is the rust-stained cliff rising above its western shore.

Leave this lake, which lies directly astride the contact zone, and pass through the low saddle just west of Peak 10,493. Continue north across the narrow strip of meadow separating Green Treble Lake from its placid eastern neighbor, then stroll into the idyllic meadows that blanket the floor of a large basin. Considering its proximity to the Saddlebag Lake Road, this fabulous cirque, with its near-perfect proportions of pine, granite, and water, remains curiously untrammeled. (A similar site in the Alps undoubtedly would contain a large hut, a network of eroded trails radiating from it, and copious quantities of trash.)

The High Route hiker next embarks on the most alpine section of the route since Blue Lake Pass. Although the crossing of the east ridge of Mount Conness is not particularly difficult, it contains all the ingredients for a thrilling adventure: firm granite, airy traverses, and stunning views. From the basin ascend north up grass-covered ramps and gullies alongside the cascading stream that originates on the ridge far above. After a gentle climb of some 800 feet—during which time there are excellent views of Mount Dana and its drab companion, Mount Gibbs—the hiker arrives at an extensive flat area at 10,900 feet. To the northeast, about a quarter of a mile distant, lies a broad, grassy saddle. But instead of aiming for this obvious gap, proceed due north up a rocky slope that ends on the east ridge of Mount Conness.

Greeting the hiker who accomplishes this short climb is a bird's-eye panorama, for he or she stands above an appalling dropoff. Below repose dozens of lakes, some of which lie directly on the contact zone between the granite and the slate. On the visible portion of Saddlebag Lake, anglers' boats scuttle about like water beetles on a pond. North Peak's amazingly sharp summit horn towers prominently to the northwest; below it lie several of the rockbound Conness Lakes. To the right of North Peak rises the serrated mass known as Shepherd Crest; the High Route soon crosses Sky Pilot Col, the saddle just to its right. Farther right, the stark ocher- and rust-colored cliffs at the head of Lundy Canyon provide another dramatic reminder that the traveler stands on the Sierra's eastern flank.

After assimilating this magnificent view, do not become discouraged when trying to pick out the next section of the High Route. The hiker's instincts rebel at the thought of descending the steep cliff below, and this proves to be the correct decision. Instead, turn west and scramble up the aesthetic east ridge of Mount Conness for several hundred feet until, at about 11,300 feet, it meets a conspicuous curving spur that drops abruptly toward the lowest Conness Lake. This providentially situated class 2 spur affords a spectacular and direct route to the lake below.

Upon leaving the ridgecrest of Mount Conness, carefully cross low-angled slabs and snowpatches until reaching the top of the curving spur. Descend this feature for approximately 700 feet to the pleasant meadows near the outlet of the lowest Conness Lake. At this point the hiker stands just above the tumultuous cascade that plunges into the basin containing Greenstone Lake.

The next High Route obstacle proves tame in comparison to the crossing of Mount Conness's east ridge. Although North Peak's east ridge must be crossed, it is surprisingly gentle, rising only a hundred feet above the creek. Surmount this rounded hump at any of several possible places and descend its steeper northern flank to the flat, rocky terrain leading north to Cascade Lake.

This pleasant site, with its striking juxtaposition of water, granite, and meadow, proves to be an excellent spot to pause and admire the effects of glaciation. The traveler need not be an expert in glaciology to discern traces of the ice sheet's passage, for they are everywhere. For instance, hundreds of glacial "erratics" cover the acres of slabs. These enormous chunks of rock, transported from afar by the moving ice, were marooned when the ice finally melted, some 10,000 years ago. Irregularly shaped patches of glacier-polished rock are visible from long distances, and these can reflect so much light that even in a region where all is brightness the traveler must quickly avert his or her eyes from the glare. By examining these glass-smooth slabs more intimately, the hiker can discover two further signs of the glacier's passage. Parallel striations show the exact direction in which the ice flowed, dragging with it pebbles of hard rock. Semicircular nicks in the granite indicate that larger stones, under tremendous pressure from the weight of the ice, preyed upon weaknesses in the bedrock, chipping fragments loose. These "chatter marks" also indicate the direction in which the ice flowed.

Cascade Lake to Shepherd Lake

From the north end of Cascade Lake follow a fairly decent path that meanders up the pleasant timberline country rising to the north. At approximately 10,900 feet the traveler arrives at a shallow tarn known as Secret Lake. Above its rocky shores it is possible to pick out the next High Route Pass, Sky Pilot Col. This gap, located immediately to the right of the talus-covered mass of Shepherd Crest, lies only 700 feet above Secret Lake. But the terrain leading upward to the pass proves far more rugged than the previous section, with talus and scree replacing grassy hillsides.

The route to Sky Pilot Col can be divided into three distinct sections. The initial obstacle, a fairly stable talus slope, involves an elevation gain of about 300 feet and leads to the bottom of a shallow bowl devoid of vegetation. Next, a stretch of ever-steepening talus leads up the left side of this bowl to the final indignity, a short but steep scree slope that most hikers will find offensive.

Sky Pilot Col, at 11,600 feet, is the highest point

reached by the High Route since Gabbot Pass. This gap on the Sierra crest is named for the conspicuous blue flower that blankets the entire saddle in midseason. The fragrant sky pilot, or polemonium, grows only above 11,-000 feet, and Sierra mountaineers long have regarded it as the symbol of the alpine zone.

As one might expect, the views from this high perch are extensive. Numerous lakes dot the foreground landscape; the largest of these is Saddlebag Lake, here seen in its entirety. Especially dramatic is the north side of North Peak, where high-angle snow couloirs slice a spectacular cliff. Far to the south, twenty-two miles distant, rises the dark horn of Banner Peak, last seen from Blue Lake Pass. Looking in the opposite direction, the viewer gazes across the glaciated trench of Virginia Canyon toward several noteworthy peaks. Most conspicuous, by reason of its coloration, is Virginia Peak; the traveler easily can see why its official name was once Red Peak (the name was changed in the mid-1950s to avoid confusion with the Red Peak of the Clark Range). Behind this rust-colored pyramid rises northern Yosemite's highest point, Matterhorn Peak. To its left lies Whorl Mountain, recognized by its steep, rugged east face. Directly in line with this prominent feature is Soldier Lake, perched on a shelf and completely surrounded by granite. The High Route soon reaches this remote body of water. In the foreground, only a mile away, the viewer can discern a portion of Shepherd Lake, the next High Route objective.

The 1,300-foot descent from Sky Pilot Col to Shepherd Lake is not technically difficult, yet the traveler cannot relax for a single step: the terrain demands constant attention. The talus, although not particularly steep, tends to be unstable, for the hiker scrambles down slate, not granite. Year-round snowfields, when soft, offer short stretches of glissading, but the sight of the sharp rocks lurking below serves as a constant reminder not to lose control, even for an instant.

During the course of this less-than-pleasant descent, the traveler almost certainly will spot flocks of tiny birds flitting about the snowfields. The gray-crowned rosy finch, one of the few birds to be found in the Sierra above 11,000 feet, roams the surface of the snow in search of insects. After observing these active inhabitants of the subalpine zone, John Muir commented that they "always have a white tablecloth for their meals."

Shepherd Lake to Stanton Pass

At Shepherd Lake the terrain changes abruptly; from a world consisting solely of rock and snow, the traveler steps instantly into a region of meadows and willows. In fact, willows so choke the stream below the lake that for a few minutes the hiker will be stymied by their wiry branches. The solution, luckily, is not hard to figure out: simply walk down the left, or west, side of the brook, keeping at least 100 feet away from the watercourse. In this manner it is possible to avoid the most sinister tangles of willow, instead traversing through normal timberline country.

When about one-half mile below Shepherd Lake, the backpacker enters a forest of hemlocks and lodgepole pines. Shortly below here, the willows begin to infiltrate the entire valley, and the traveler realizes that it is time to flee; the High Route, after all, is not a jungle trek. At about the 10,000-foot level, cross the stream and angle to the right. Head in the direction of Gray Butte, the rocky cone of granite seen across Virginia Canyon. The next mile to the floor of this canyon proves remarkably straightforward. Proceed down gentle terrain through open stands of pine, occasionally dropping down short, steep inclines. Wildflowers, especially lupine, cover the hillsides; corn lilies and paintbrush line the verdant margins of the side streams. The area is obviously an ideal habitat for another plant, the rarely seen Leichtlin's tulip. More commonly called the mariposa lily, this striking wildflower can be recognized by its snow white petals, which display a splash of yellow and black at their bases.

Still aiming for Gray Butte, the traveler eventually emerges onto the wide floor of Virginia Canyon, one of northern Yosemite's most dramatic features. After crossing two major streams (the hiker should be able to find stream-spanning logs over these), step across the Virginia Canyon Trail and begin a long ascent up the opposite side of the canyon. Enormous lodgepole pines block the upward view, but Gray Butte sometimes can be glimpsed high above; head for its left edge. The terrain steepens gradually, as might be expected on a scramble up the side of a U-shaped valley. But at 10,200 feet the angle eases, and hikers suddenly find themselves moving through sublime timberline country, following a brook that rushes down massive slabs of granite.

During this wonderful section the traveler is surrounded by numerous varieties of wildflowers, including penstemon, heather, and phlox. This region of broken slabs also is overrun with pikas, small mammals whose nasal, two-syllable alarm calls fill the air as the hiker approaches. This distant cousin of the rabbit—heard far more often than it is seen—spends its entire life in the boulderfields. The observant hiker probably will discover large piles of dried, or drying, grass stored under overhanging rocks. Oddly enough, the pika does not hibernate; the gathered "hay" sustains the big-eared animal during the winter months, which are passed in underground chambers.

After completing a total ascent of 1,400 feet from Virginia Canyon, the High Route traveler arrives at Soldier Lake, a circular body of water nestled tightly inside a textbook example of a cirque. A clump of whitebark pines clings to the eastern shoreline of the lake, adding to the charm of the locale. From the lake's outlet ascend a rounded ridge and then a shallow, whitebark-lined gully to the broad saddle west of Gray Butte. Reaching this saddle the hiker sees, only one mile away, mighty Virginia

Peak, its reddish upper half looking oddly alien in an otherwise normal landscape.

The High Route's next goal, Stanton Pass, lies in plain view to the left of Virginia Peak, and the route to it is most obvious. Simply diagonal over to it, keeping above a group of lovely tarns. Slabs, then talus, can be followed until meeting a system of class 2 ledges that end on the wide pass separating Virginia and Stanton peaks. During this final stretch to the saddle, aim for a small notch seen near the highest whitebark pines on Stanton Peak's ridge.

A tremendous panorama greets the traveler who settles onto the windswept col. Back to the southeast, the viewer can discern Sky Pilot Col, the minuscule pass recently surmounted. Behind it, far in the distance, rise the uppermost few feet of lofty Mount Dana. Most spectacular, however, is the cluster of alpine summits only six miles distant: Mount Conness and its satellites. Looking west from Stanton Pass, the traveler gazes straight across the glacier-carved trench of Spiller Creek Canyon toward Whorl Mountain, an orange-hued peak of singular beauty. To its right rises Matterhorn Peak, and farther right still, somewhat below the viewer's level, reposes the final watershed boundary of the High Route—Horse Creek Pass.

Stanton Pass to Twin Lakes

The descent from Stanton Pass can prove tricky if the hiker does not find the easiest possible route. The most logical place to leave the pass seems to be near a notch marked by the uppermost whitebark pines (mere ground-hugging shrubs at this altitude) on Stanton Peak's ridge. Leave the ridgecrest and drop down the rocky slope a few yards until confronted with a steeper section. The next 100-odd vertical feet are class 2–3 in difficulty; scout the route carefully before making any major decisions. The exposure, while not extreme, is such that unsteady hikers should relinquish their packs to more experienced persons. Alternately using narrow ledges and loose gullies, wander downward, remaining on the flanks of Stanton Peak rather than on the cliffs directly beneath the saddle. Numerous variations exist in this area. In short order the traveler reaches the relative security of a talus slope.

Descend this talus until the terrain levels out near the highest pines visible below. From this welcome resting spot the hiker begins a much easier section—the diagonal traverse to the floor of Spiller Creek Canyon. After reaching the creek the traveler encounters few problems while heading upstream toward the obvious gap known as Horse Creek Pass. The brook tumbles down meadowlands blanketed with wildflowers, and, above, the cliffs of Whorl Mountain seemingly overhang the valley floor. The High Route is rarely more pleasant than during its final mile on the western slope of the Sierra.

Horse Creek Pass, at 10,650 feet, lies just below Matterhorn Peak, the enormous talus pile named by the Wheeler

Survey in 1878. Lincoln Hutchinson, who made the first ascent in 1899 with his brother James and two others, considered the aptness of the peak's name in the *Sierra Club Bulletin:* "That the name is a poor one there can be no doubt, for . . . there is only the barest suggestion of resemblance to the wonderful Swiss mountain after which it is called. Yet the name is of so long standing that it seems hardly best to think of making any change."

The final few miles of the High Route prove relatively straightforward, for the traveler follows a single watercourse—Horse Creek—from its source to its demise in the marshes at the western end of Upper Twin Lake. For the first few miles the terrain is rough, involving snowfields and talus. But below the flat canyon floor at the 8,500-foot level, the hiker picks up an excellent path that winds down forested country on the east side of Horse Creek. During this section, the trekker comes suddenly upon several extensive beaver ponds, the only ones seen along the High Route. Beavers were introduced long ago to certain streams on the east flank of the Sierra, but a limited supply of aspens—their favorite food—has kept the mammals from flourishing.

At the 7,800-foot level the traveler joins a maintained trail on the east side of Horse Creek. After a mile-long descent, during which several species of conifers will be noted, the High Route trekker reaches the valley floor only a few hundred yards from civilization.

Reversing the Route

Hikers who begin their High Route adventure at Twin Lakes must locate the trail leading toward Horsetail Falls. This marked path begins in the southern suburbs of the resort area called Mono Village. After crossing Robinson Creek and then Horse Creek, the trail begins switchbacking up the forested hillside to the south. When the trail reaches a conspicuous flat section of valley above Horsetail Falls, pick up an excellent path leading up Horse Creek Canyon.

At about the 9,600-foot level on Horse Creek the traveler must veer right, paralleling the row of colorful pinnacles extending outward from Matterhorn Peak. By doing so, Horse Creek Pass can be reached without any further routefinding problems.

The exact point where the traveler leaves Spiller Creek Canyon is unimportant; the object is simply to reach Stanton Pass, the conspicuous saddle just right of red-topped Virginia Peak. On the final stretch to this pass keep far to the right, on the flanks of Stanton Peak.

From Stanton Pass the hiker easily can spy Gray Butte, rising only a mile or so to the southeast. Aim for the flat saddle to its right, then drop down past Soldier Lake to the floor of Virginia Canyon. During this descent study the next High Route obstacle, Sky Pilot Col; it lies near the head of the major canyon seen directly across the glacial trench. The pass also is visible from the outlet of

Shepherd Lake; the correct notch lies just right of a huge, squarish block that leans to the right.

The traveler encounters no further routefinding problems until reaching the environs of Mount Conness. From the outlet of the lowest of the Conness Lakes ascend south up a prominent rounded spur leading to the east ridge of Mount Conness. When nearing this imposing ridgecrest, avoid the temptation to traverse left too soon, for steep snowfields lurk here until late season. Instead, continue upward until it becomes safe to move left onto the ridgecrest.

Drop east down this crest for a few hundred feet, then leave it and head south down gentle country until reaching the tree-covered basin far below. Continue south across superb timberline country to the broad saddle overlooking Spuller Lake. Here the traveler obtains an excellent vista of the next section of the High Route. More or less directly in line with Mount Dana, and about one-and-a-half miles away, lies an inconspicuous, reddish-colored knoll. The next High Route col—Mine Shaft Pass—can be seen just right of the knoll. During most of the traverse to the pass, the red knoll is superimposed upon Mount Dana, thus simplifying the routefinding.

From Mine Shaft Pass curve south half a mile to the crest of the Sierra, a wide pass marked by the ruins of Summit Mine. From this historic site the hiker should have little trouble finding the correct route down to the Tioga Pass Highway.

Alternate Routes

The topography of this part of the Sierra dictates that the High Route follow a fairly rigid course. In fact, only one alternate route is obvious: the bypass of Sky Pilot Col. Although this variation is less direct and involves stretches of bushwhacking, it also avoids a significant section of talus—a fact that some hikers may appreciate.

Leave the High Route a few minutes after passing Secret Lake and work up and left along a series of class 2 ledges until reaching the extreme northern end of the half-mile-long saddle stretching between North Peak and Shepherd Crest. From this 11,200-foot saddle a well-defined path winds down 700 vertical feet to the beautiful meadowlands a quarter of a mile northeast of Upper McCabe Lake.

Leave the path at the meadows and strike west, soon dropping down a willow-choked valley toward McCabe Creek, located in the prominent wooded canyon far below. Leave the creek at the 9,700-foot level and climb a gentle slope up and right to the low, wide saddle northeast of Peak 10,085. From this pass work diagonally down through a dense forest until reaching the floor of Virginia Canyon. The High Route is joined a mile or so upstream, when almost under the cliffs of Gray Butte.

Mountaineering en Route

Lembert Dome

Lembert Dome is not only one of the most attractive features of the Tuolumne Meadows region; it also offers the hiker an easy climb capped by a superb view. On a summer's day the climber is likely to share its rounded summit with numerous other adventurers, for the prominent formation lures hikers from the nearby campground. The dome was named after John Baptist Lembert, a hermit who in the late 1880s homesteaded a small parcel of land surrounding the soda springs just west of the dome. At this idyllic site Lembert raised angora goats until a severe winter depleted his stock; afterward, he collected butterflies and botanical specimens for museums. In 1896 Lembert was murdered by a robber at his winter quarters below Yosemite Valley.

The top of the dome can be reached quickly from the vicinity of the Tuolumne Meadows High Sierra Camp. Follow the marked trail toward Dog Lake until reaching a ridge several hundred feet above the Tioga Pass Highway. Leave the path here and stroll west through open woodlands to the massive granite slabs that make up the summit area.

Gaylor Peak

Another easy-to-reach landmark offering a fine view is Gaylor Peak. This 11,004-foot mass, composed of reddish slate, is climbed most easily via its gently angled south ridge. Lying less than one mile from Tioga Pass, it too is likely to have a teeming summit on a midafternoon in August.

Mount Conness

As the highest crest peak north of the Tioga Pass Highway, Mount Conness naturally offers the climber a sterling viewpoint. All of Yosemite's significant peaks are readily identifiable, and on a clear day the viewer can distinguish the massive shape of Mount Goddard, sixty-eight miles downrange.

Clarence King and James Gardiner of the California Geological Survey made the first ascent of this lofty landmark in 1864, naming it in honor of United States Senator John Conness. To reach this eminence, leave the High Route near the extensive flat area one-half mile south of the peak's east ridge. Work up the rocky terrain to the west, keeping well above Alpine Lake. At the 12,000-foot level, join the east ridge and scramble up a few hundred feet of class 2–3 rock to the summit plateau.

Shepherd Crest

Shepherd Crest, while not a particularly handsome mountain, proves so easy of access from the High Route that its ascent should be considered by all adventurous hikers. From Sky Pilot Col the outing involves only 400 vertical feet of class 2 talus.

Peak 10,800+

Located just south of Soldier Lake, Peak 10,800+ cannot be considered a bona fide mountain climb. But those who accomplish the ten-minute stroll from lakeside will be rewarded with a disproportionately fine view. Mount Conness, displaying its extensive glacier, dominates the skyline to the southeast. To the south, the jagged spires of the Cathedral Range rise from the forested landscape. Farther west, the viewer also can distinguish the upper portion of Half Dome, some twenty-three miles distant.

Stanton Peak

Another peak lying in close proximity to the High Route is Stanton Peak. A class 2 talus ridge leads to its top from nearby Stanton Pass; the ascent involves an elevation gain of only 500 feet. From the summit the hiker obtains a unique view of the great glacial canyons of northern Yosemite.

Matterhorn Peak

The traveler can follow in the footsteps of Jack Kerouac and Gary Snyder by ascending Matterhorn Peak from Horse Creek Pass. Although the ascent is not technically difficult, the climber will discover—as did Kerouac—that the loose terrain often proves annoying. From northern Yosemite's highest summit the viewer gazes across thousands of square miles of wilderness, though the more interesting view is that of the Sawtooth Ridge, lying just beneath one's feet. Towering rock walls rise from sparkling white icefields, and ridges sweep upward to culminate in airy summits. For half a century this pristine alpine landscape has been considered a rock-climber's paradise, and on a summer's afternoon, as cumulus clouds begin to form, the climber well may hear yodels of victory resounding from the nearby crags.

Index

H U M P H R E Y S

BM 10844

Summit
Lake

Creek

1600

Piute Pass 11423

Golden Trout
Lake

11169

11200

BM

Piute

ksaddle
Lake

B A S I N

8

Paine Lake

Wahoo

Muriel
Lake

S I E R R A   N A T L   F O R E S T

12498

Lakes

12127

Em

11600

Lost
Lakes

12873

Goethe L

12000

Muriel
Peak

GLACIER

12000

12971

12942

Alpine Col

The Keyhole

Goethe Glacier

12400

FRESNO CO

INYO CO

DIVIDE

Mt Goethe

10800

12355

12000

12000

Darwin

Evolution

Canyon

11600

McClure
Meadow

Evolution   Valley

12000

10000

Colby
Meadow

13385

10885

10000

10993

11200

13691

Mt
Mendel

10800

Darwin

Creek

VABM 1383

Evolution
Lake

Mt Darw

Canyon

10400

McGee

12360 The Hermit

12000

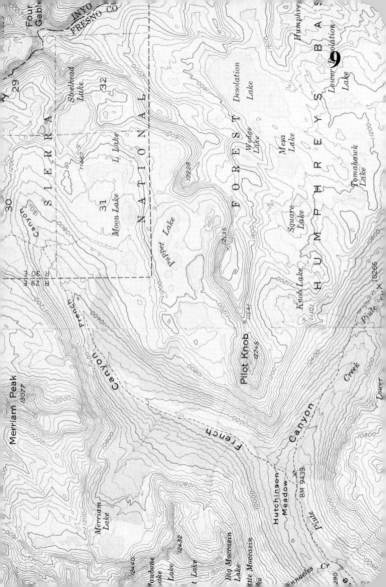

11

Creek

9200

11667

Frog Lake

11600

Third Recess Lake

Third

Recess

12406

12356

Snow Lakes

12267

12145

Fourth

13198

12691

Second

Mills

FOREST
BOUNT

11646

Creek

Lower Mills Cr Lake

Recess

Mt Mills
13468

rst Recess

1200

Upper Mills Cr Lake

Mt Ab

N
O

Mist Lake

12836

1400

12692

Mt Gabb
13711

DIVIDE

L

Hilgard Lake

Toe Lake

Mt Hilgard
VABM 13361

12800

Lake Italy

12546

11154

Hilgard

Italy

Jumble Lake

Garnet

Nydiver Lakes

Ediza Lake

Iceberg Lake

Cecil

Minarets

R A N G E

Banner Peak
12945

Mt Ritter
13157

12344

Lake Catherine

Mt Davis
12311

North

Twin Island Lakes
9988

Ste

Bench Canyon

Canyon

Bench

Electra Peak
12442

NDARY

19

Evelyn Lake

Tuolumne Pass

Boothe Lake

Creek

Upper Fletcher Lake

Townsley Lake

Vogelsang High Sierra Camp

Fletcher Peak

Creek

Hanging Basket Lake

Vogelsang Lake

R A N G

Emeric

Vogelsang Peak

Gallison Lake

TUOL

Creek

Bernice Lake

MARIPOSA CO.
MADERA CO.

Lewis

11659

Florence Cr.

9600

Florence Lake

Florence Lake

Florence

Creek

9600

9200

10800

Mt Florence
12561

10867

Cony Crags
10539

MARIPOSA CO
MADERA CO

9200

10000

10800

11647

10000

22

Excelsior
Mtn   12446

15   14   I N Y O
                                                                        13
        Shepherd
        Lake

10945   0800

                                                                              Lundy
                Creek   Falls

                Shepherd   Crest   N A T I O N A L   Falls   Mill
    Creek   24
                            10000   23
                                    22   Falls
                                          12015
                                                                Falls

                                        Lake Helen

                                                        Shamrock   Lake
Upper McCabe   27   Hess   Odell
        Lake   Mine   26   Twin   Lake   25
McCabe Lakes   28   Lake
                                    Steelhead Lake   Lundy Pass
                            10800   "Z" Lake   Hummingbird
                            Cascade Lake   Mill   Lake

                                        Wasco Lake   I N Y O
        Sheep   33   North Peak   35
        Peak   34   Greenstone   36
                                    Conness Lakes   Lake
                                                                        Saddlebag
                    T 2 N   Conness   10400
Roosevelt   T 1 N   Glacier
    Lake   Conness   N A T I O N A L
                            VABM   Saddlebag
                            12590   Campground
                                        Alpine   Carnegie Institute
                                        Lake   Experimental Sta
                                                                        Sawmi
                                        MONO CO   Campgrou
                                    Green Treble   Maul Lake
                                        Lake   F O R E
                                    Big Horn   Finger   Spuller Lake
                                        Lake   Lake
                            White Mtn   Fantail
                                                                    Lake

23

East Lake

Nutter Lake

Gilm...

Hoover Lakes

TUOLUMNE CO.

INYO

TOIYABE

Burro L...

Epidote Peak

Page Peaks

Gabbro Peak

East ...

9767

9200

Glines Canyon

T 3 N

T 2 N

Summit L

MONO CO.

Onion Lake

Excelsior

Camiaca Pk

11739

Virginia Pass

Creek

Canyon

Twin Peaks

Gray Butte

12893

Soldier Lake

Stanton Pk

12200

Virginia Pk

11200

1695

1529

Spiller Lake

Whorl Mtn

12029

Creek

Spiller

10800

9800

P A R K

10000

9696

24

Mono Village

TWIN

Creek

N A T I O

Creek Falls   6
Falls

Creek Falls

8857

9200

R 23 E
R 24 E

Cattle

8800

Blacksmith

9600

Horse

10007

8

Crai
1394

8400

Creek

8600

10875

ier Lake

Avalanche L

Creek

10800

9600

The Cleaver

1181

9600

awtooth

11200

10827

Ridge

10000

Lake
Frances

Glenb
Lake

Turquoise
Lake

9600

B

12264

Matterhorn
Peak

11200

Burro
Pass

inger Peaks
1390

10800

P

11200

Twin Peaks

10000

Whorl Mtn
9,2029

10000

11200

1237